How to Get the Job You Want in a Law Firm

Also available from Wiley

*GOING TO LAW SCHOOL?: EVERYTHING YOU NEED TO KNOW
TO PURSUE A CAREER IN LAW*
by Harry Castleman and Christopher Niewoehner

*THE COMPLETE LAW SCHOOL COMPANION: HOW TO EXCEL AT
AMERICA'S MOST DEMANDING POST-GRADUATE CURRICULUM*
by Jeff Deaver

*TAMING THE LAW SCHOOL DRAGON: HOW TO SURVIVE
AND THRIVE IN FIRST YEAR LAW SCHOOL*
by George Roth

How to Get the Job You Want in a Law Firm

Ann Turnicky

Illustrated by Eugene Theroux

John Wiley & Sons, Inc.

New York • Chichester • Weinheim • Brisbane • Singapore • Toronto

For Ron, as ever

Library of Congress Cataloging-in-Publication Data

Turnicky, Ann
    How to get the job you want in a law firm / Ann Turnicky : illustrated by
Eugene Theroux.
      p. cm.
    Includes bibliographical references and index.
    ISBN 0-471-15742-2 (pbk. : alk. paper)
    1. Law—Vocational guidance—United States.   2. Law firms—United
States. I. Title
KF297.T875   1997
340'.02373—dc21   97–21708

Printed in the United States of America

10 9 8 7 6 5 4 3 2 1

CONTENTS

ACKNOWLEDGMENTS

The scope of experience reflected in this text is the result of contributions from many experienced recruiting professionals in the legal and nonlegal community. Regretfully, there are too many people in the recruiting world who have directly or indirectly contributed to this book to mention everyone by name. But I must thank the staff at the National Association for Law Placement in Washington, D.C., for their assistance on this project, especially Julie Hamre. NALP opened up their offices to me and gave me access to tremendous amounts of information on several occasions. To them, I am indebted.

Several attorneys and staff members at Baker & McKenzie's Washington, D.C., office also unselfishly assisted me on numerous occasions. In addition to giving me a place to call home for over five years, the personnel at Baker & McKenzie helped me as I labored on this project even after I had departed the firm. Special thanks go to Ken Hodges, Eugene Theroux, and Joe Andrus.

I also have to thank Sue Williams, who over the years has taught me the importance of dedication to an endeavor, no matter how large or small. I know, Sue, it's in the details. I give her credit for much of what I know.

And last, but certainly not least, I must give a special thanks to Patricia Gallagher. Pat lent me her insight, wisdom, and experience, and she pushed me and made me realize that this book could, in fact, become a reality. I couldn't have done all this without her unselfish help and motivation.

PREFACE

There are only the pursued, the pursuing, the busy, and the tired.
—F. SCOTT FITZGERALD

When I decided to write this book, I realized that I had spent almost one-third of my life working in law firms. Obviously, I enjoy my profession even though law firms can often be all-absorbing places to work. If I had to do it all over again, I wouldn't change a thing.

It's ironic, and probably not coincidental, that *attorney* is the Latin word for "actor." As you go through the law firm recruiting process, you'll discover that some attorneys would make excellent actors. It has also been said that many impressionable undergrads decided on a legal career only after having become entranced with *L.A. Law* in the 1980s and John Grisham novels in the 1990s. But to secure a position today in a law firm requires more than a familiarity with the weekly television lineup or a glance at the *New York Times* bestseller list. If you think the legal world bears any resemblance to *L.A. Law,* hold on to your hat. Law firm life isn't for the fainthearted. It's a rough world out there. But there is an exhilarating spirit that suffuses law firm life that is difficult to understand until you experience it for yourself. It is an environment of intellectual stimulation, akin to working in academia, but in the corporate world. Few professions require the mental horsepower and toughness found in the legal world. I feel quite fortunate to have spent so much of my time working in such a unique environment.

But do not be misled. Law firm life isn't for everyone, and not all of its members are academic intellectual giants, or even interesting, for that matter. For every Sandra Day O'Connor, there is an ambulance-chasing charlatan who has hurt, more than helped, the profession. At its worst, the legal profession allows greed to overtake gentility; it reduces this honorable *profession* to nothing more than a *business.* Just pick up a newspaper or read the legal press. There are endless accounts of licensed attorneys who have overstepped their bounds and let the mighty dollar misguide their actions and warp their judgment.

As I did the research for this book, what I found most interesting is the difference between the personality of the typical law student and the personality traits needed to secure a job in a law firm today. While I'm overgeneralizing a bit about the law school or law firm personality, it is undeniable that the legal profession attracts many academic, intellectual types, many of whom would prefer to research case law than learn how to market themselves to potential employers.

So how do law students and practicing attorneys learn the marketing-related techniques needed to land a job in a law firm today? Learning to market yourself is a key component in your job search. In today's legal job market, you need to be able to play offense and defense equally well; you have to be adept at both marketing yourself for your career and performing up to very high standards from the time you begin law school to the end of your legal career. While this theme will come up more than once as you read stories of others who have already traveled down the law firm recruiting path, I'm not going to attempt to solve this dilemma. What I will do is lend you my years of experience in law firm recruiting to help point you in the right direction. I believe that if you know how the recruiting process works inside law firms, you will be better prepared on the outside.

Caveat emptor. Before you board the law firm *Titanic*, try to map out where you want to head your ship. And make sure you know what you're getting into. Life is too short not to use some kind of compass, especially as an associate in a law firm. But even more important, do what you enjoy, and if law firm life can fill that void, as it has for me for many years, chart your course and have a successful journey. And a few acting lessons probably won't hurt. *Bon voyage.*

INTRODUCTION

Working in a law firm can be intensely exciting, intellectually stimulating, and financially rewarding. It can also be stressful, boring, and frustrating. The key is to find the best job in the best firm for you at every stage in your legal career, from finding the best summer associate positions to changing jobs as an associate. But for all of its ultimate rewards, trying to find a job in legal America today is tough no matter who you are, where you came from, or what you wanted to be when you grew up.

The process of finding a job in a law firm is still evolving and hasn't yet reached a settling point. It's a completely different world today than it was even ten years ago. In today's law firms, baby boomers and generation Xers, with divergent outlooks on life and work, are working side by side. It's a world in which diversity—which the legal world is still struggling to deal with successfully—is becoming the norm, not the exception. It's a world in which loyalty is increasingly rare. And it's a world in which billable hour requirements and associate profit margins are now written down. The genteel legal profession, where law was considered a profession, not a business, can now only be read about in Charles Dickens's novels.

While that assessment may sound pessimistic, the truth is that finding a job in a law firm today is difficult. The statistics bear this out. According to the National Association for Law Placement, the governing body of the legal recruiting profession, of the 39,199 graduates from American Bar Association–accredited law schools in 1995, of graduates for whom legal employment was known, 86.7 percent found legal-related employment. But of that 86.7 percent, only 56.1 percent went into private legal practice at a law firm. This contrasts sharply with the 92.0 percent legal employment rate for graduates in 1988, of which a peak of 64.3 percent went into private practice. The number of students entering private practice has steadily declined. What's more, the median starting salary for attorneys has fallen in recent years, while the tuition rates for most law schools—and default rates on student loans—have risen exponentially.

The good news is that in the last few years the overall number of graduates entering law schools has started to decline. The factors of supply and demand are beginning to influence even the sacred bastions of legal academia. But a shrinking pool of associate talent probably won't make it that much easier to enter the walnut-paneled walls of the exclusive clubs we call law firms. Like the rest of the service-based American economy, law firms have taken a beating in recent times and have been forced to operate more efficiently, like the businesses that they have become.

But lawyers at all levels continue to find good professional positions. And law firms, both large and small, that have weathered many storms in recent years and have done their share of downsizing are continuing to look for entry-level as well as experienced attorneys. I believe that even in today's hypercompetitive work environment, law firms are still good places to hang your hat. Law firms, large and small, pay their attorneys very good salaries, which are the envy of many professions. It just takes a little more "know-how" to find the right place to plant your roots.

In this job market, you have to know what you're looking for, and you have to plan ahead. You can't sit still and wait for the right job to come along, because it never will. You can't depend on someone else's efforts to find you a job—*you have to do the work.* You have to be persistent and dedicated, and you have to want it *badly.* And most important, you have to feel good about all of the decisions you make during the recruiting process. I've seen too many people make job-related decisions that didn't coincide with what they really wanted out of life and work. Do it right on the front end so you won't have to fix it on the back end.

That's the point of this book—to help guide you through the maze so that you can make well-informed, well-planned, and well-executed decisions about getting a job, any kind of job, in a law firm. I'm not going to supply you with any secret answers or gimmicks. I'm simply going to lend you my recruiting experience in these pages, with the hope that it can help you along the way.

HOW TO USE THIS BOOK

This book contains six parts, arranged according to where you are in your legal career. Since only a few sections of the book will apply to you at a time, you'll want to refer to those sections that apply to the particular stage of your legal career.

Part I will tell you how to get a law firm summer job as a first-year law student. Chapter 1 lays the groundwork for how to go about getting a first-year summer position. You'll learn why firms hire or don't hire first-year students, the importance of grades, and when you should start contacting firms. Chapter 2 gives you the basic tools you'll need, such as how to create a good resume and cover letter and when you should mail and follow up on your resume. The rules for the legal recruiting industry, established by the National Association for Law Placement, are also discussed in this section.

In Chapter 3, you'll find specific information on how to land a position once you obtain interviews. You'll learn how to dress properly for interviews, how the interview process works inside a firm, how to prepare properly for the interview, how firms evaluate candidates, how to follow up with firms, and what you should do before you accept an offer.

Part II is the largest section of the book. It deals with getting a summer position as a second-year law student. The basic elements of the second-year job search are discussed in Chapter 4. You'll learn how to assess your goals, establish a timetable for your job search, and narrow your focus geographically and by areas of practice. As in Chapter 1, you'll find out how to create a good resume and cover letter, but with special tips specifically for second-year students. This chapter also discusses how to contact firms that may or may not be sending recruiters to your school. Chapter 5 describes some of the issues that are important to understand before you go to on-campus interviews, such as why firms go to certain schools, how to get your resume selected for interviews, and hints to help you prepare for on-campus interviews. In Chapters 6 and 7, you'll learn about the ins and outs of the on-campus and in-house interview process. If you are interested in working in a small firm, refer to Chapter 8, which discusses second-year hiring in small firms. If the "typical" recruiting path doesn't work for you, Chapter 9 outlines other options that may get you into a firm. Part II ends with Chapter 10, which deals with summer associate job offers.

Part III gives you information on surviving and excelling in summer programs. Chapters 11 and 12 offer general advice on how to be a successful summer associate and discuss the operational aspects of summer programs.

Part IV is for third-year students who are still looking for a law firm position. Chapter 13 discusses putting together a resume and cover letter and how to do this successfully even if you haven't received any job offers. Chapter 14 offers advice on where to look for new associate positions.

In Part V, you'll find the resources you'll need to secure a position as a lateral or practicing attorney. Chapter 15 discusses the mistakes lateral candidates often make when looking for new positions and how to avoid them. Marketing yourself as a lateral candidate is the focus of Chapter 16. Using legal search firms and overcoming being terminated or laid off are also topics in this chapter. You'll learn how to create a lateral resume and cover letter in Chapter 17, and in Chapter 18 you'll learn how the lateral recruiting process works in firms. Partnership and economic issues are discussed in Chapter 19.

Part VI is for anyone interested in the many nonlegal positions at law firms. Chapters 20 to 22 discuss the variety of nonlegal positions available in firms today and how to go about landing a position. The last chapter of the book touches on the future of law firm recruiting.

PART ONE

GETTING A SUMMER JOB AS A FIRST-YEAR STUDENT

Mistakes are the usual bridge between inexperience and wisdom.
—PHYLLIS THEROUX

1

LAYING THE GROUND-WORK FOR YOUR FIRST-YEAR JOB SEARCH

"You can see my professors never joined the stampede to grade inflation."

The banker Walter Wristen once said that good judgment comes from experience and that experience comes from bad judgment. Unfortunately, most first-year law students have little experience searching for a job, so their judgment is extremely limited. Surviving three years of law school leaves little time to learn the tricks of the trade necessary to become successful in today's competitive legal job market. First-year students lean into the job hunt head against the wind with the huge handicap of inexperience. Three years later graduation rolls around, and only then, if ever, does the average law student know how to secure a position in a law firm. Many law students believe that because they were successful undergraduates, securing summer associate and post–law school employment will be a piece of cake. And the most common mistake students make during the job search is relying too much on their placement director or career services office to get a job. But there are steps you can take to avoid this naivete as your law firm job search gets under way. It will be much easier for you if you map out your search from the beginning.

ESTABLISH YOUR JOB SEARCH TIMETABLE

Timing is everything. I know you've heard that adage before, but first-year law students, like their more experienced peers, will fare better in their job search if they pay attention to a timetable. It is vital to understand when, as well as why, you should perform specific tasks related to your job search. Here's the basic job search timetable for you as a first-year student:

First-Year Job Search Timetable

Date	Task
Late November or early December	Prepare resume
Early to mid-December (after exams)	Begin researching firms
Christmas break	Visit firms in your hometown
Late December to mid-January	Mail resumes to major firms
Three weeks later	Follow up with major firms
January to March	Interview with major firms
March to May	Concentrate on smaller firms

Not surprisingly, recruiting professionals report that each year first-year students begin contacting law firms earlier and earlier. You should know that this tactic does not really give you an advantage; in fact, it often does just the opposite. First-year hiring decisions are usually not made until all second-year offers have been declined or accepted, which often takes until the end of December. And without grades or significant work experience, it is difficult to select one applicant over another at the first-year level. Most recruiting professionals, who by late fall are exhausted, usually do not appreciate a first-year student trying to outmaneuver his or her classmates by not abiding by the National Association for Law Placement's rules. With the supply of first-years greatly outweighing demand, "getting in early" has little significance in this job market. If anything, this tactic sours recruiting professionals and creates a negative first impression.

Don't wait too long, however, to begin contacting firms, either. Ideally, you should concentrate on preparing your resume and looking for job opportunities immediately after first-semester exams, sometime around the winter holiday break. When you contact a firm and they tell you that "hiring is complete," this message does not mean that you waited too long to contact that firm. It means that the firm probably hired only second-year students. For clarification, ask the firm if first-years were hired.

Mail your resume in December or early January. Don't wait until spring to begin your job search, as the hiring process can often take several months. When dealing with small firms, it is likely that you will have to follow up more than once or wait a month or two later to mail your resume. Small firms typically wait to determine their hiring needs closer to the summer months.

TARGET THE FIRMS THAT
WILL HIRE YOU

First-year students should be optimistic, but realistic, about their job search. It is very difficult for a first-year student to receive an offer for a summer associate position. You may be the one to beat the odds and land a coveted position in a major law firm, but you shouldn't count on it. A recent sampling of the first-year class at a top-twenty law school showed that with 308 of 400 students reporting, only 25 percent got jobs in firms. Of that 25 percent, only 2 percent worked in major law firms. But even more revealing was the fact that only 13 percent were paid more than $600 per week. (Large firms' salaries typically range from $1,000 to $1,800 per week.) The majority of law students, 45 percent, reported working for no pay. The placement director at this law school reported that these statistics have been typical of her first-year classes for the last several years. Career services offices all over the country paint similar pictures.

Let's face it, everyone wants to think that they can work for the highest-paying, most prestigious firms in the country. But you can get the jump on your fellow students if you **begin** your search on a realistic note and contact only those firms that **realistically** will hire you. Concentrate on those firms from the start; don't wait until the end of your search to get grounded in reality. You'll save a lot of time and money by seeking out firms in your hometown and smaller firms that may be interested in a zealous first-year student. Don't even contact the major firms unless your resume is truly exceptional. While your colleagues are busy collecting rejection letters from the prestigious firms in the major markets, you'll be knocking on doors that will be more likely to be opened for you. By the time your peers have become tired of rejection, you'll be going for interviews or may have even landed a position.

The experience of a former University of Michigan student stresses how "reality bites." A native Russian-speaker, his goal as a first-year was to work in an international law firm with the possibility of going to a firm's Moscow office. His mass mailing, which centered on firms with international practices having a Moscow office, was focused and targeted, but produced not even one phone interview. He soon realized that no firm was going to send a first-year (even with a good record from the University of Michigan) to Russia for the summer, even on a volunteer basis. He soon came back down to earth and subsequently targeted smaller firms in his home state, Michigan. He ultimately landed a position with a reputable local firm and had a very successful summer. But he had to readjust his expectations, his focus, and his attitude to make it all work. His advice to aspiring first-years is be realistic and stay focused with lower expectations, making sure that your attitude matches the adjustment.

WHY FIRMS HIRE FIRST-YEAR STUDENTS

As you map out your job search plan, it is useful to understand the pros and cons of hiring first-year students from a law firm's point of view. You may be able to target some firms based on their past history of why and how they decided to hire first-year students.

The Pros

It's an accepted fact in most law firm circles that first-year students aren't hired to lessen the workloads or increase the billable hours at busy law firms. First-year students aren't known for their efficiency. They simply don't have enough training at this point in their legal career to work efficiently on major projects. But since many firms continue to hire first-years, there must be a good reason.

Some firms fill holes in their summer programs with first-year students. If a firm budgeted to hire fifteen students but had acceptances from only twelve, then the remaining three spots may be filled with first-year students. While you aren't privy to the hiring statistics at law firms, you may be able to find out which firms had an unusually poor showing at your law school. You may also be able to find out which firms are being "blacklisted" by student groups for whatever reason. Look for those firms that may not be in favor with the students.

Two other common reasons firms employ first-years are to improve the quality of the students they hire in the future and to broaden their hiring base by reaching out to schools with which they may have had little success in the past. One large Texas firm decided to hire first-years from top-ten schools outside of Texas as a way to broaden the firm's hiring base. Yale and Stanford students, for example, have less trouble securing summer employment as first-years than do students from less prestigious schools. Many firms reach into the first-year classes at the top schools to improve their success rate when recruiting second-year students at those schools.

Some firms hire clients' sons or daughters as first-year law students, in the belief, often mistaken, that this practice is a viable client development tool. This exercise is risky if it backfires and can create more negative feelings than positive results. Occasionally, however, this practice works well for all parties involved. One firm hired the daughter of someone who had referred a lot of work to the firm. She came from an excellent school and had a great summer experience. Not only was she ultimately hired as an associate, but she simply loved the firm and acted as an ambassador at the school for the firm. The recruiting efforts at her school tripled in the years following her first summer. Everyone was happy. Similarly, hiring a neighbor's daughter or re-paying a favor to someone by employing their best friend's son for the summer is a practice utilized occasionally in firms. Don't be afraid to network, using whatever connections you may have to your advantage.

The Cons

As I mentioned earlier, first-year students aren't known for their efficiency. But more important than that (especially since even second-year students are not considered efficient and aren't usually hired to churn out billable work) is the fact that it's difficult to keep track of and continually recruit first-year students as they progress through the second and third years of law school. Most first-year students don't end up working for the firm that employed them during their first summer. Many first-years, who are happy to get any law firm job, accept positions with firms in which they have no genuine interest. They need something, anything that looks good, to put on their resume, even if they hate the work, the people, or the location. Most associates didn't begin their legal career at the firm for which they clerked as a first-year student.

THE IMPORTANCE OF GRADES

The significance of law school grades, especially during the first year, cannot be overemphasized. Many law firms, especially the large ones, rely almost completely on law school grades to screen resumes and, in many cases, to make hiring decisions. Just because you have a stellar undergraduate record doesn't mean that you are assured of a spot in a law firm. As one placement director from a Midwest law school stated, "It is a painful shock to realize that class rank will limit employment options." The truth is that if you have been accepted to a law school, it's a given that you have an impeccable undergraduate record or you wouldn't be there. But a solid undergraduate record will not guarantee that your law school grades will be good. Many excellent students with impeccable undergraduate records struggle through law school.

One Washington, D.C., law school revealed that one of its students, a Fulbright scholar, ended up at the bottom of her class after her first year of law school. Thoughts such as "If they would just meet me, they would change their minds" are of no avail. Many law firms have established criteria that students must meet, fully realizing but ignoring the fact that most law students are bright and have strengths that may not be apparent on a resume. *Grades matter more than anything else.* A small minority of students are able to overcome mediocre grades, but that's not the norm.

Prior to receiving first-semester grades, some law firms will hire first-year students on the basis of their undergraduate records. As the number of first-year students being hired has declined, this practice is becoming less common. One can only imagine what the resumes of these students look like—Rhodes scholars, perfect undergraduate records, top athletes, very unusual and sought-after work experience, multiple language capabilities, and so on. For example, one first-year who was hired on the basis of his undergraduate record was a Top Gun pilot, was a former member of the U.S. ski team, and attended a very prestigious law school. Screening the resumes that come through law firms can be a humbling experience. Don't depend on your undergraduate record unless your resume is one for the record books. While it is possible to enter a firm this way, it's not probable.

Remember that your number one priority, as your law school placement director has no doubt already told you ad nauseam, is to complete your first year of school with as strong a knowledge base as possible. If you fail to grasp the basic legal concepts taught that first year, it usually shows up later. Moreover, it is important to remember that much hinges on a good first-year grade point average. Most students don't realize how important this is. No amount of interviewing can compensate for low grades, unless you can manage to defy the law of averages.

2

THE BASIC TOOLS FOR YOUR FIRST-YEAR JOB SEARCH

"My keenest interests? Foreign trade! Litigation! Taxation! Intellectual property! Trusts and estates! Pro bono work! I'm into all of it!"

The first step in your successful job search is to assemble the basic tools you'll need. Your toolbox should contain a good resume, a cover letter tailored for each employer, a firm grasp of the basic rules of the industry (in our case, the National Association for Law Placement), effective mass mailing techniques, and an understanding of when to contact firms, how to use networking effectively, and how to use an informational interview properly. Without these tools, your job search will take you all over the map. Every action should be planned carefully and then executed. The skills you learn here can be applied throughout your legal career.

One more tip as you prepare for your first-year job hunt: Buy an answering machine before recruiting gets under way. Recruiting professionals become frustrated attempting to reach students who don't own one. It's just too difficult to reach you if you don't have one. Once you set yours up, make a habit of calling in to check your messages during interview periods if you want to expedite the interviewing process.

THE FIRST-YEAR RESUME

The "art of the resume" is one of the most important elements of the job search process and one of the least understood. Many people do not know how to create a good resume and spend large sums of money with "resume experts," who often know less. Who better than you knows your strengths, weaknesses, and accomplishments and can put them down on paper? Creating a good resume is simply a marketing exercise—marketing yourself on paper to multiple audiences in order to land a job.

Utilize the years of career service expertise in your law school's placement office. Placement professionals are well versed in resume preparation and can provide you with multiple models that can help you design your own. Many law schools also sponsor resume writing workshops at least a few times each year. You can refer to the sample resume on the following page as a guide.

Format

One of the keys to a successful resume is a concise format. Most recruiting professionals spend less than 30 seconds reviewing a resume. Yours is possibly one of hundreds being reviewed during the same sitting. If you can't glance at your resume and instantly pick out the important points, then chances are that yours will not make it beyond this review. It is also vital that your resume be error free. Most recruiting professionals will automatically throw out a resume with a typo or misspelled word. Make sure at least two people other than yourself review your resume for mistakes. Reading a resume backward, from the bottom to the top, is a good way to discover any errors or typos.

Your resume should be one page in length. Your educational background should be presented first, followed by your work history, specific technical skills, language skills, and personal interests.

Printing a resume on expensive paper is not necessary. In fact, some expensive heavy paper will not feed through a copy machine. You should use a higher grade than plain copy machine paper, but don't break the bank. Most recruiting professionals will pay little attention to expensive watermarked paper. Also, avoid using dark colored paper, such as gray or dark tan, since even light gray paper doesn't always copy well. Since you want your resume to be photocopied and passed around for many people to review, make sure it is easily readable and easily duplicated.

Take a look at the sample resume again. Note that it is clear and concise—you can quickly glance at it and pick out all of the relevant points. Always set in **boldface** the main elements like your law school, your undergraduate

First-Year Resume

Emma L. Smith
1588 Beacon Street, Apt. 8
Boston, MA 02142
617-352-5666
e-mail: emmalsmith@aol.com

Education

HARVARD LAW SCHOOL, J.D., expected 1997
Captain, Intramural Softball Team
Volunteer Coordinator—Legal Service for the Elderly

EMORY UNIVERSITY, Atlanta, Ga., B.A., History, 1994
Summa cum laude, Phi Beta Kappa
Varsity Tennis Team, Departmental Thesis Award
Personally financed 75% of college expenses with part-time and summer jobs.

Salem Academy, Winston-Salem, N.C.
Graduated 1990, Valedictorian

Experience

Summer
1994

U.S. China Forum
Washington, D.C.
Research Assistant
Organized and administered Chinese educational programs for visiting dignitaries. Performed related research and translated documents from Chinese to English.

Summers
1990–1993

Wellington Smith, C.P.A.
Charlotte, N.C.
Accounting Assistant
Worked in family-owned accounting practice. Performed general office functions, set up new computer system, trained personnel, negotiated contracts with vendors.

Other
Experience

Attended intensive eight-week course in Mandarin at Middlebury College in Middlebury, Vt., summer 1994. Worked as a tour guide in France for six weeks, summer 1993. Have also worked as a waitress, tennis coach, and computer programmer to help finance college and law school expenses.

Interests/Skills

Fluent in French and Mandarin Chinese. Familiar with WordPerfect, Excel, and Lotus. Interests include tennis, Chinese art, and community service.

References and writing samples are available upon request.

school, and your previous employers. Be careful not to put in bold points that will come off as obnoxious. For example, if you have a good grade point average or if you have won coveted awards, don't set them off to bring them to the reader's attention. A seasoned recruiting professional or someone genuinely interested in your candidacy will know where to look for those items.

Grades

Employers want to see grades on resumes, but only undergraduate and law school grades, if available. A good rule of thumb is to include your grades if your average is above 3.0 or its equivalent. If your grade point average is below 3.0, you should be aware of the message you might be sending if there is no indication of your grades anywhere on the resume. One recruiting coordinator at a large Texas firm stated that first-year resumes are not even considered if there are no grades from law school or undergraduate school. Nevertheless, I recommend the 3.0 or higher rule.

Personal Interests

Most people who do a lot of recruiting like to see personal interests on a resume. Include two or three lines listing your hobbies, but make it interesting, and be specific. For example, if you are a history buff, include a specific interest, such as "Civil War history" or "nineteenth-century Russian history." This adds a personal touch to your resume and creates a topic of conversation during the interview process. Many times I've remembered a candidate by making a mental note of his or her unique interests. One student included "zymurgy" as a hobby on his resume. Since it baffles astute attorneys to see words they've never heard of, this fact alone helped him to get multiple interviews. Almost every person he spoke with asked him about his strange-sounding hobby. "Zymurgy" is simply the science of fermentation, and this clever student expressed his interest in this field by brewing beer!

Other Helpful Resume-Building Hints

Make sure you include the geographic location of your past jobs. Don't assume that a potential employer will know the location of your past employers, especially if you worked outside a major metropolitan area. Include only significant educational honors unless you need items to fill the page. Don't include every job you have had since you were 15 unless significant or really out of the ordinary. If you've held multiple summer jobs while in college, indicate that without being too specific. Instead of listing every fast-food restaurant you've worked in or every country club where you've been a caddy, state only that you held multiple summer jobs, such as waitressing, lifeguarding, retail clerking, and so on. The important point is that you worked or did something productive during those years.

Include computer and language skills only if you are proficient at the time you are preparing your resume.

First-Year Resume Do's and Don'ts

Here is a quick list of do's and don'ts that you should review as you prepare your first-year resume:

Do's

- Do make your resume one page in length.
- Do make it concise with wide margins.
- Do write in present tense for current items and in past tense for past items.
- Do include location of jobs and schools (include city and state).
- Do list grade point average if over 3.0 or the equivalent.
- Do include computer and language skills.
- Do list your college major (and minor if you have one).
- Do include personal interests—be creative about it.
- Do attach a transcript if yours is good (use the 3.0 rule for undergraduate and law school).
- Do use 8½-by-11-inch paper, standard letter size.
- Do use only black ink.

Don'ts

- Don't spend money on "resume experts."
- Don't misspell words or have typos.
- Don't abbreviate—spell things out completely whenever possible.
- Don't include educational history before college or include every job you've had since you were 15 unless very significant or needed for filler.
- Don't list numerous educational honors unless significant.
- Don't include language skills unless you're fluent when the resume is prepared.
- Don't list "relevant" courses.
- Don't print your resume on colored paper.
- Don't list actual references—indicate that they're available upon request.
- Don't include a writing sample—if employers need one, they'll ask for it.

THE COVER LETTER

Your cover letter should do three things:

1. Introduce the reader to the resume
2. Highlight specific points in the resume
3. Include information that may not be on the resume

Your cover letter should not be longer than one page in length and, ideally, should consist of only three or four paragraphs. Some recruiting professionals review cover letters only after they skim and become interested in a resume, while others always read them, whether they like the resume or not.

Recruiting professionals say that cover letters often reveal which students have done their homework. Cover letters are an excellent way to distinguish your strong writing skills by demonstrating your ability to express yourself succinctly and concisely. This skill may not be apparent on the resume. One recruiting coordinator stated that she automatically throws out resumes when the cover letter is too pat or too dry. She routinely looks for interesting vocabulary in cover letters. Another hates to see students expound on what they expect the firm to do for them in the cover letter. Statements such as "I am interested in your firm because of its well-known trial advocacy program" should be avoided. While the statement demonstrates that you have done your homework, it sounds self-serving. She would prefer to see the student talk about what he or she can do for the law firm.

Format and Presentation

Your cover letter should be dated and include a complete address, telephone number, and e-mail or Internet address. Indicate where you can be reached if you aren't at your mailing address for an extended period of time. Your letter should be formal (address it to "Ms." or "Mr."), and you should sign it using your first and last name. Make reference to your resume in the body of the letter, and attach it with a paper clip. Also state that you will follow up with a phone call in a few weeks to ensure that the resume was received. See the sample cover letter on the following page as a model.

Common Mistakes

When preparing your cover letter, make sure that you avoid some of the mistakes recruiting professionals routinely see on cover letters. The pointers on page twenty are some helpful hints, garnered from years of experience, that may help guide you.

First-Year Cover Letter

1588 Beacon Street, Apt. 8
Boston, MA 02142
617-352-5666

December 1, 1995

Ms. Emily R. Rogers
Recruiting Coordinator
Hall & Levitz
390 West Fifth Street, N.W.
Arlington, VA 22206

Dear Ms. Rogers:

As a first-year student at Harvard Law School, I am seeking a summer associate position, preferably in the Washington, D.C., area, where my grandparents live. I have already made arrangements to live with them this summer so that I can work for a firm and do volunteer work with the D.C. Chapter of Legal Counsel for the Elderly. My resume is attached for your review and consideration.

At this point in my legal career, I am simply anxious to obtain some legal experience in a law firm in an area of the country in which I want to work. I have a strong undergraduate record and have already spent some time in the Washington, D.C., area. As you may know, Harvard holds exams after the winter holiday break, so my grades will not be available until early spring.

I plan to be in Washington in mid-December for interviews and would welcome the opportunity to talk with someone at your firm about employment possibilities. I will call and follow up in a few weeks. Hopefully, we can set up a meeting at that time. In the interim, I can be reached at 617-352-5666.

Thank you, in advance, for your consideration, and I look forward to talking with you.

Sincerely,

Emma L. Smith

1. *Don't misspell a firm's name.* Even simple names are butchered on cover letters. This kiss of death for many applicants demonstrates a complete lack of attention to detail. This can land your resume in the wastebasket in record time.
2. *Avoid the "goofed mail merge."* This is when a cover letter is addressed to the wrong firm at the right address; for example, a letter to Baker & Botts contains the address of Baker & Hostetler. This is a common occurrence, especially during the fall, when students mass mail hundreds of resumes. When a firm receives these cover letters, the recruiter won't know whether the student is interested in their firm or the other one, especially if the firms are distinctly different. Or maybe the student doesn't really care.
3. *Don't address your cover letter to a recruiting coordinator who left the firm four years ago.* This plainly demonstrates that you have not done your homework.
4. *Don't mention practice areas that the firm doesn't work in.* For example, never assume that every firm has a litigation practice, because they don't. Students routinely include inaccurate information about practice areas in their cover letters because they have not done their homework.

Surprisingly, these mistakes are common, and recruiting coordinators report that they receive cover letters with these errors almost every day. To the receiver, these mistakes demonstrate an acute lack of attention to detail. If you're going to make these mistakes, just save your postage stamps.

ADDRESSING AND MAILING YOUR COVER LETTER AND RESUME

Always address your letter to the company's recruiting coordinator. If you don't know her name, utilize the Directory of the National Association for Law Placement (NALP). Your career services office has this directory. If a firm doesn't have a recruiting coordinator, send it to the personnel director, hiring partner, or office administrator, in that order. If you have the time and money, call each firm, and get the right person's name.

Some people prefer to mail their resume to a partner who attended their law school. I'm not in favor of this practice for several reasons. First, it may slow down the entire process. For instance, if that attorney is out of town for two weeks, your resume will just sit on his desk during that time. Chances are that when he receives it, he'll just forward it to the recruiting coordinator, anyway.

It makes little difference to busy recruiters if you fold your resume and cover letter and mail it in a regular white envelope or whether you double or triple your mailing costs by mailing your resume flat in a brown letter-size envelope. It's likely that the package will be opened by a secretary, anyway. You shouldn't be mailing enough paper as a first-year student to warrant the extra expense. Staple or paper clip all your sheets together so that when the envelope is opened, everything is in its right place.

Always type the envelope with a return address, or use mailing labels. It's so much quicker, and it just looks so much more professional than a handwritten address. This also eliminates the problem of someone not being able to read your handwriting, thus delaying the delivery.

Don't be surprised if you don't receive a response from the firm. Even some large firms don't respond to first-year inquiries anymore, simply because they don't have the support staff in place or because the cost of mailing responses to hundreds or even thousands of inquiries has become so high.

MASS MAILING YOUR RESUME

Mass mailing—mailing large quantities of your resume to employers at large—is the method of choice in the law school recruiting process, at least from the perspective of law students. But mass mailing is expensive and wasteful and does not usually yield good results. The majority of students don't land a job using this method. For example, Baker & McKenzie's Washington, D.C., office typically receives approximately one thousand first-year resumes each year, usually between the months of December and February alone. If the office even interviews first-years, five students might be selected to interview—0.005%! So save your postage stamps. If you are going to mail your resume to potential employers, do so selectively. Target firms that realistically will hire you, as discussed in Chapter 1.

FOLLOWING UP ON YOUR RESUME

Follow up with firms with a phone call two or three weeks after you send your resume. It can often take more than a week for a resume to reach its destination. Some recruiting professionals only read resumes once a week, so you should also allow for that. Also, keep in mind when you call that since firms receive often hundreds of resumes each week, the chance of someone immediately remembering yours is remote. You may find that calling the large firms is a wasted effort, since it is unlikely that you will get hired there using this method. Following up with the smaller and local firms is a much better use of your time. While some large firms have computer-based tracking systems for resumes, you might have better success obtaining interviews with follow-up calls to smaller law firms simply because the number of applications is smaller.

When you make your follow-up calls, indicate who you are and that you recently sent in a resume, and ask if the firm is still hiring first-years. If the answer is yes, ask when you can expect to hear from them about the possibility of an interview. If you are planning to be in the area for interviews, tell them just in case there is an interest in talking with you and the firm does not want to pay for travel expenses. If the firm is not hiring, ask if they know of anyone who might be hiring. The operative word here is *networking*.

THE IMPORTANCE OF NETWORKING

As a first-year student, you don't possess large chunks of free time to reinvent the wheel. One fundamental component of any job search strategy should include networking. Networking is vital to any job search in the 1990s. No one leaves home without this skill anymore.

Even a stellar first-year candidate may have to utilize the "N word" to get into a law firm in today's market. Most first-years get jobs not through mass mailings, but through personal contacts. One Washington, D.C., law school reported that in its 1994 first-year class, 37 percent got jobs using personal contacts, the highest percentage of any method, while only 1 percent found positions through mass mailing. Networking involves using everyone you know to find out which firms are hiring and how to get interviews at the ones that are. Your closest relatives do not have to be partners in big firms to open the magic doors for you, either. Remember, everyone, including law students, has connections; the trick is to know what they are.

Networking 101

Networking is not a skill taught in law school classrooms. Here's a good way to begin the process of networking:

1. *Make a list of ten people you would call if you needed solid business advice.* This list can include even brief acquaintances. Then add to this list everyone you personally know in the business community who has any connection with a law firm. Your list should include aunts, uncles, neighbors, your friends' parents, professors, and so on. Be creative. Stretch to include friends of friends or even casual acquaintances. This is how you begin networking.

2. *Contact the individuals on your list by phone.* When you call, tell them who you are, bring the individual up to date with your current situation, and then explain why you are calling. Never directly ask the person on the other end for a job. Simply inquire whether they know of anyone who might be willing to employ you, even for free, over the summer or if they know anyone who might know of a lead. At the very least, you may be able to set up several informational interviews, which may lead to something else. Eventually, your calls will not be cold but will be built on references from other people. You will be calling Thomas Mitchell because his friend at the Ski Club, William Elder, suggested that you call him.

3. *Be persistent.* You will discover that people genuinely like to help bright students who are eager to work. Many people in today's corporate environment have been in your shoes and will be sympathetic to the difficulties of a job search. And if you have ever done a favor for someone else, start calling in your chips. People you have helped in the past may feel inclined to help you now. The worst thing that can happen during this process is that someone will say "no." And if you are uncomfortable with rejection, you should get used to the concept as you begin your legal career.

   You cannot give up because you have not yet yielded results. One first-year student literally opened the Washington, D.C., and suburban Maryland yellow pages and started calling law firms, starting with the *A*'s, in order to land a summer job. After making hundreds of calls, he came across an attorney who was so impressed with what he was doing that he hired him for the summer. This fact impressed many law firms at which he interviewed as a second-year student, as well, and ultimately helped him land a job in a law firm. Persistence pays off in the long run.

4. *Learn to integrate networking into your everyday life.* Networking is also about being involved and getting out into the community, and it is a skill that is essential, especially for an aspiring attorney. Individuals looking for a long-term career in a law firm will have to learn the art of networking at some point. Learning how to talk to strangers in business and social settings is a skill that is invaluable as a budding associate or young partner. Collect business cards, and join organizations that get you outside the law school environment. These tips may sound like goals only experienced attorneys set for themselves, but you should start thinking about developing and honing these skills now, even as a first-year student.

INFORMATIONAL INTERVIEWING AS A JOB SEARCH TOOL

Informational interviewing in law firms—interviewing attorneys to gain information about a firm or a particular area of law—is an excellent resource you should tap into as you begin your job search. While these interviews are not intended to yield job offers, they assist you in creating a network for job hunting now and in the future, allow you to hone your interview skills, and teach you a lot in the process.

SETTING UP THE INFORMATIONAL INTERVIEW

Busy attorneys are often turned off by requests to take an hour out of their day to talk with law students about their practice and law firm, so it is important to approach them in the right way. Don't just pick up a legal directory and start calling attorneys, seeking to line up informational interviews. You must first do a little homework.

1. *Focus on one or two major practice areas first.* Consult your personal contacts, law professors, and people you may have met while networking who practice in the areas you are interested in pursuing. If, for example, you have an interest in environmental law, ask a professor if he or she personally knows anyone in this field with whom you could talk.
2. *Get your contact to make the initial phone call.* Then you follow up a few days later, setting up a time for the interview.
3. *Use your local bar association as a resource.* Call them and ask for directories of attorneys who practice in areas that interest you. Ask them if you can attend one of their meetings. Remember that you may have difficulty getting a busy attorney who has no connection to you to grant you an informational interview. You must network a little bit!
4. *When you interview the attorney, do some prep work.* Know enough about the area of practice to ask substantive questions. Do some background work on the attorney as well, flattering him or her to a degree. Interest is the sincerest form of flattery, but make an effort to sincerely thank the attorney for agreeing to talk with you.

The purpose of the informational interview is not to get a job but to educate you about an area of practice, a particular law firm, and interviewing in general. Do not forget this during the interview. *Always* follow up with a thank-you note immediately after the interview, and thank the person who helped you secure the interview, as well. Remember, everyone you meet becomes part of your network, so always be professional.

LAW FIRM RECRUITING STANDARDS AND PROCEDURES

The National Association for Law Placement, more commonly known as the NALP, is the governing body and watchdog of the law firm recruiting industry. NALP's membership is composed primarily of law school placement personnel, law firm recruiting professionals, and law school deans. NALP's members work together to establish common rules and guidelines that promote fair and equitable practices in the legal hiring arena.

To help facilitate equitable recruiting practices in the industry, NALP's members have established a set of principles and standards for the timing and acceptance of job offers. A copy of these guidelines is included in the Appendix. While not all law firms are members of NALP, the association's guidelines are widely recognized as the industry standard. It is important that every law student understand these principles and adhere to them, since most law firm recruiting activity is modeled on these guidelines. In addition to understanding what applies to the student population, it is equally important to appreciate how the standards apply to law firms. Firms, like students, are sometimes caught manipulating the guidelines to suit their needs.

If you are a first-year student, pay particular attention to Part V, Section D of NALP's guidelines. NALP rules state that law schools are not supposed to offer placement services to first-year students before November 1, except in the case of part-time students. This means that no employers or students should initiate contact before December 1 and that offers to first-year students for summer employment should remain open for at least two weeks after the date the offer is made.

Small firms are more susceptible to breaking NALP's guidelines, especially regarding keeping offers open for at least two weeks. One firm, for example, offered a position to a first-year student, giving him only 48 hours to make his decision. He had other interviews lined up and wanted to fulfill his obligations and talk to these firms. Fortunately, he was able to move up his interview dates and put off the firm long enough to review his options. He ultimately accepted another position.

If you are caught in this situation, you should handle it with kid gloves, attempting to foster good relations with the law firm, while also trying to get a job. Small firms often do not have the luxury of making offers to multiple students, so they often need to know very quickly if you are coming on board or not. You need to learn how to handle these situations as they occur. Your placement director is an invaluable resource for advice if you find yourself in one of these sticky situations.

There are good reasons for adhering to these guidelines that restrict first-year job-seekers to the winter months. Placement offices are inundated in the fall with second- and third-year students and simply do not have the resources to handle first-year requests during this busy time. Law firm recruiting professionals face a similar scenario. But the most important factor is one that has already been mentioned: First-year students should focus all of their energy on simply getting through the first year of law school and getting the best grades possible.

3

LANDING THE JOB: THE FIRST-YEAR INTERVIEW

"I'm set for the summer, Mom. A thousand bucks a week to knosh
at barbecues with the partners!"

First-year interviewing can be a terrifying experience. You always hear the folktales about the student who interviewed all morning with his fly open or her slip hanging out from underneath her dress or about the person who referred to a firm by the wrong name. One student at the University of Pennsylvania had over twenty-five initial interviews in a two-week period. He was so exhausted and tired by the end of the second week that he couldn't remember firms' names any longer. During an on-campus interview, he told the partner he was interviewing with that he couldn't recall his firm's name, but he knew it was unusual. The attorney quickly replied, "Can you say Brown & Wood?" Needless to say, he didn't receive a callback.

Nervousness is expected of first-years. But be careful not to come across as too slick or too rehearsed. Learn to be natural during the process—be yourself. And since the majority of first-year interviewing is now performed in-house from the start, you have the luxury of meeting attorneys in their environment for the first interview instead of having to interview in a dark, windowless basement room in an obscure law school building. So breathe deeply and learn from the experience.

HOW TO DRESS FOR INTERVIEWS

When dressing for interviews, be extremely neat and tidy in appearance, and always err on the conservative side. Shoes should be shined, your shirt pressed, collar stiffened, socks matched, pantyhose clean and smooth, purses businesslike, and hair neatly combed and cut. Don't forget to check your breath! Briefcases are optional for both men and women, and you should *always appear* organized. Surprisingly, interviewers pick up on every little detail, and details do make a difference.

For Women

Women should wear suits or simple dresses with jackets. I'm not an advocate of the navy blue suit syndrome—the belief that only navy suits are appropriate for interviews—but suits should be simple in nature and conservative in style, avoiding bright colors, such as bright blue, red, lime green, or yellow. Blouses should never be low-cut. Pantyhose should be nude, beige, or matched to the suit (i.e., black hose with a black suit). Wear minimal jewelry such as simple pearl or diamond earrings and a watch. Save your perfume for other occasions. Keep your hair off your face completely. Keep makeup to a minimum, and always avoid bright-colored nail polish. If ever in doubt, opt for the conservative.

For Men

Men's suits should be made of lightweight wool (not polyester) and preferably single-breasted, although there is nothing wrong with a fashionable European double-breasted suit for interviews in the larger metropolitan areas, such as New York and Los Angeles. I'd advise wearing dark colors, preferably gray. Stay away from brown. Shirts should be all cotton, ties silk, and shoes should be leather wing tips or loafers, with socks to match. Earrings should be left at home. During inclement weather, wear a neatly tailored raincoat. Borrow one if you have to.

Remember that many law firms, large and small, often give the appearance that they are bastions of right-wing, conservative views, which is often reflected in an unspoken dress code. Whether you agree with the practice or not, it's always better to err on the side of the conservative when you are trying to make a positive first impression. Remember, this is not the time or place to make an outspoken fashion statement.

HOW THE IN-HOUSE INTERVIEW WORKS

The first-year in-house interview is akin to a five-year-old's first day of school. It's natural to be apprehensive, eager, and terrified all at the same time. You won't know what to expect, no matter how prepared you may be. At the other end of the spectrum, experienced lawyers don't always know what to expect or ask of first-year students when interviewing them, either. Most cannot remember (or don't want to remember) what it was like to be a first-year student interviewing in a law firm for the first time. For these reasons, most first-year in-house interviews are awkward at best. I always reminded the lawyers I worked with not to be amazed at a first-year's awkwardness or lack of questions. It isn't a reflection of their intelligence or potential. Law schools simply don't teach students what to expect during the first round of first-year interviews. And like most activities, you get better with practice. Interviewing is an art that must be mastered.

Preparing for the Interview

Here are the steps you should take to prepare for your interview:

1. *Plan your day in advance.* This includes knowing where your interview will take place, how long it will take you to get there, knowing what you're going to wear, having your briefcase packed, and making sure that you get to bed early the night before.

2. *Always arrive fifteen minutes early for the interview.* Find the building before the day of the interview, and know where readily available parking exists. If, for any reason, you are running more than fifteen minutes late, stop and call the recruiting coordinator or the office administrator, if possible. It's far better to take the time to call rather than to give a negative first impression by being late. And a "no-show" is an unforgivable sin. There is simply no reason why someone should fail to appear for an interview without calling the firm.

3. *Always bring extra copies of your resume, transcripts, and writing samples to the interview.* Sometimes resumes are lost or misplaced, and this will make you appear one step ahead of everyone else. Also bring a writing tablet (preferably with a leather or vinyl cover) to take down names and brief notes, if necessary. Even if you do not need these items, you will appear prepared and eager to learn about the firm.

4. *Read the local and national newspaper the night before your interview and again the next morning.* This supplies you with current topics for conversation should the interview get slow, and it demonstrates that you

are well-read and informed. If you have the time, scan a few well-respected magazines for additional conversation topics.

5. *Review any materials you may have on the firm.* This might include marketing materials from your placement office, articles from legal publications such as The *National Law Journal* or The *American Lawyer*, or information from the legal directory *Martindale-Hubbell.*

Who'll Be There

Typically, in a medium-sized or large firm, you'll interview with four to eight attorneys. In small firms, you might talk only with one or two attorneys. Firms handle in-house interviews in various ways and select interviewers using different criteria. Partners and associates usually interview at this level, and frequently the hiring partner will be involved. Nevertheless, firms roll out a portion of the red carpet for first-year students. Interviews last anywhere from 15 minutes to 45 minutes each, and often students are treated to lunch or dinner at a nice restaurant. The entire process should take anywhere from one hour to half a day, depending on the firm.

You'll be escorted around the firm, sometimes by the attorneys themselves or by a staff member. At many firms, the interviewing attorney will escort you to the next interview. If you are not given a tour of the firm, ask to see the offices, the library, and the rest of the facilities. Learning about what the various firms offer in terms of facilities and staff will help make your selection process easier as a second-year student. Use this time to help prepare for next year.

Often, first-year interviewing is not given the same level of attention as second-year recruiting. Firms have less information to go on (i.e., often no grades). Moreover, it is proven that retention rates with first-year students are lower than with second-years. Also, by December or January, after the second-years have come through, attorneys are very tired of interviewing law students. So do not take what may appear as a blasé attitude from the attorneys personally.

HOW FIRMS EVALUATE FIRST-YEAR CANDIDATES IN-HOUSE

There's no magic to evaluating candidates for law firm positions, especially at the first-year level. In fact, the process is so unscientific that it would baffle management consultants unfamiliar with law firm terrain. In large firms, often the hiring committee, seated around a large conference room table, reviews evaluations and comments, and decides which candidates to hire. In some firms, especially the smaller ones, the decision is made by one or two people. In one large, well-known boutique firm, the recruiting coordinator and hiring partner make all first-year hiring decisions. Never take for granted whom you're dealing with during the interview process, as you never know who's calling the shots when it comes to hiring.

Candidates are evaluated by the interviewers, and evaluation forms are completed and turned over to the recruiting coordinator or personnel director for permanent possession. Firms often have their own evaluation forms. The National Association for Law Placement also has a generic form that many firms utilize. Remember that lawyers are not known for putting intangible "gut" feelings about other people down on paper. My experience has shown that the real feedback is garnered during meetings, when these topics are discussed "off the record."

Some firms require a partnership vote on all hiring matters, while others leave the decision up to the hiring committee based on the planning needs of the firm. And there are many "undocumented" cases of rogue partners making the sole decision to hire a candidate (usually a distant relative or the son or daughter of a client). This is a recruiting coordinator's nightmare, and it happens more frequently than not. (This is when networking works for the law student but backfires on the recruiting coordinator.) The "insider trading" method is a frequent unwanted vehicle for first-year hiring but is a way in the door for those students with strong law firm connections or superb networking skills.

Firms evaluate first-year candidates mostly on the three Cs: connections, congeniality, and craving (i.e., they like you). If you're hired by a law firm as a first-year, chances are you meet at least one of these criteria. Second-year hiring gets a bit more scientific and sophisticated.

FOLLOWING UP WITH FIRMS
AFTER INTERVIEWS

Politeness is still valued by law firms, and I encourage you to send thank-you notes to the firms with which you interview, either to the recruiting coordinator or to one of the attorneys with whom you interviewed. It's not necessary to send a letter to everyone with whom you interviewed, especially if you spoke with several people. A good rule of thumb is if you interviewed with five people or less, send a note to everyone. Otherwise, send a thank-you note to one attorney, asking him or her to forward a copy to the others, or address your letter to the recruiting coordinator, asking him or her to do the same. These letters are often circulated around the firm, so again, make sure you use paper that is easily read when photocopied.

SUMMER ASSOCIATE EVALUATION FORM

SUMMER ASSOCIATE _____ DATE _____

SCHOOL/YEAR _____

EVALUATION: Please complete and return to Ann Ogburn as soon as
             possible.

(Rate from 5–0, with 5 being the best)

	5	4	3	2	1	0
Ability to anyze legal problems						
Quality of research						
Writing skills						
Verbal facility						
Creativity						
Cooperation						
Timeliness on projects						
Professional judgment and maturity						
Potential						

Rank this person in relation   RECOMMENDATION
to other summer associates:
                                      Recommend for employment   _____
Outstanding   _____
Above average   _____   Not recommended   _____
Average   _____
Below average   _____   Did not get to know well enough
                                      to make a recommendation   _____

COMMENTS: _____

_____

_____

SIGNED _____ DATE _____

Proofread your letter for errors before you mail it! You can interview all day long, but sending out letters with typos or misspelled words can end your chances faster than a speeding bullet. I can't stress enough how important it is for you to pay attention to the details. There is also the dilemma of whether to send a personal, handwritten note or a typed, business-style letter. A handwritten note is certainly more informal and personal, while a typed letter is more generic and formal. Personally, I prefer a handwritten note simply because it's more interesting, revealing, and more personalized. Use your best judgment, and choose whichever you feel more comfortable with based on your preference and the impression you have of the people to whom you're sending the note. Probably, the larger the firm, the more formal your approach should be. No matter which method you use, if handled correctly, sending a thank-you note can only help you.

Don't wait too long to send the thank-you note, especially if hiring decisions are being made quickly. The note should arrive within a week of your visit to the firm. This is also an ideal time to include any promised information such as transcripts or references. Your letter should be brief, one page in length. See the sample letter on page 34 for a model.

TRAVEL REIMBURSEMENT FOR INTERVIEWS

Most firms do not reimburse first-year students for travel expenses. **Never** assume that you are being reimbursed. Ask the recruiting coordinator or office administrator if you need clarification. If you're fortunate enough to be reimbursed for your travel expenses, send your expense form in promptly. Usually the recruiting coordinator or office administrator will give you a reimbursement form at the interview. Make sure you sign the form and date it, and always include receipts (for accounting purposes).

If you have any questions about what is reimbursable and what is not, call the recruiting coordinator for clarification before the expense is incurred or, at the very latest, before you mail in your form. See the sample reimbursement form on page 36. Remember that each firm has a different policy and approach regarding travel expenses. Follow these policies to the letter.

Job Offers

If you're fortunate enough to receive job offers from law firms as a first-year student, count your blessings. You're definitely in the minority these days. But no matter who you are and how many job offers you may receive, there's a right and a wrong way to handle the process. Even if you don't have multi-

Thank-You Letter

1588 Beacon Street, Apt. 8
Boston, MA 02142
617-354-5666

February 15, 1995

Ms. Melissa Ann Warren
Bell, Book & Candle
617 First Avenue, Suite 899
Washington, DC 20006

Dear Ms. Warren:

I want to thank you for taking the time out of your busy schedule to speak with me last Thursday about a possible summer associate position with your law firm. Few firms that I have visited gave me the strong impression that yours did, from the friendly receptionist to an entertaining lunch with Bill Dudley and Jason Woodward.

I was particularly impressed to learn that your firm routinely works on Section 482 matters in the tax area. Although, as a first-year, I have not taken any tax classes yet, this is an area that I am interested in, due primarily to my exposure to tax through my family's accounting practice. The firm's other areas of practice, trade and intellectual property, also interest me.

If I can provide the firm with additional information or references, please do not hesitate to contact me. Your firm appears to be an inviting place to work, and I would welcome the opportunity to spend a summer there. I look forward to hearing from you.

Sincerely,

Elizabeth A. Lawrence

ple offers waiting in the wings, let this exercise be a warm-up for your second-year interview season. Learn early in your career the right and wrong way to make these decisions. Too many students burn their bridges very early on, simply because they didn't take the time to turn down or accept job offers in a polite and timely manner.

Before You Accept

If you receive a summer job offer from a law firm, there are several points you should consider when making your decision. If dealing with large firms, make sure the firm gives you at least two weeks to make a decision, in accordance with NALP guidelines. Firms sometimes take liberties with first-years and cajole them into making quick decisions, since it's in the firm's best interest to know immediately if you are coming on board or not. With the tight job market for first-year students, some firms think they can get away with this practice. It's not unreasonable to ask for additional time if you are dealing with a large firm, so do so if you need to.

Occasionally, firms try to manipulate students on salary issues. It is common for firms to pay first-years less than second-year students, but the gap shouldn't be significant. One large East Coast firm wanted to hire a few first-years but decided to pay them one-half of the second-year rate. It is acceptable to ask firms what the second-year salary is when they quote you the first-year rate. Your placement office may also possess this salary information. While you may not be in a position to demand higher wages, you don't want to enter a situation in which you feel slighted, which might cause negative feelings the entire summer. Fortunately, this isn't a common practice.

Make sure you find out what your job responsibilities will be. Don't assume that you'll be given legal research to perform or that you'll be doing the same work as the second-year students. Ask what your responsibilities will be if this hasn't been made clear to you.

Get It in Writing

Always request that your job offer be sent to you in writing. While a summer associate offer will not be as complex as that of a regular associate receiving benefits and vacation pay, you should have some things spelled out on paper. This will eliminate any uncertainties and will back up what you have been told in the interview process, should there be any problems or miscommunications later on.

One such horror story involves a student who received an offer from a small New York firm over lunch in January. When he reported to work in June, to his dismay, he discovered that his salary was $250 a week, not the

BELL, BOOK & CANDLE
Washington, DC

TRAVEL EXPENSE REIMBURSEMENT FORM

It is our policy to reimburse reasonable travel-related expenses incurred during your interviewing trip. If you have questions about what constitutes a reasonable expense, please call Ashley Smith for clarification before incurring the expense.

Name: _____

Address: _____

Phone: _____

E-mail Address: _____

Names of other employers visited on this trip and contact person at each (check contact who is receiving original receipts). Use the letters by employers' names to indicate below which employer is responsible for each charge.

Employer/City	Date	Contact
(A)		
(B)		
(C)		
(D)		

Please check one of the following options:

_____ No other employers were visited on this trip.

_____ I have sent this form and receipts to only you because I understand that you have agreed to bill other employers for their share of expenses.

_____ I have sent copies of this form and receipts to all prospective employers listed above and have indicated each employer's share of expenses. Your share of expenses is $_____ payable directly to

_____ at _____

Signature _____

Date _____

$1,000 he was originally quoted. He also spent his first week at the firm photocopying files instead of doing legal research, as he was told. He was informed that he could take the job or leave it, and the firm denied ever promising to pay him $1,000 a week or promising him that he would perform legal research.

To eliminate potential problems, the letter should state your job title and briefly define your responsibilities, job function, and salary. If the firm has a policy on summer start and end dates, those dates should also be included in the letter. Keep a copy of the letter for future reference. Again, shafting first-years is not a common practice in law firms, so don't be alarmed. But it's always a good idea to have a paper trail. It's also a good practice to begin your career by developing a professional eye for proper business procedures.

THE WAY TO A SUCCESSFUL SUMMER—SOME BASIC HELPFUL HINTS

There are lots of things you can do to assist your transition to law firm life, even if only for a summer. You should be prepared to make some mistakes as you adjust to law firm life, but you can make that adjustment run smoothly if you follow some of my advice. Law school doesn't do the best job of preparing you for this transition, so don't be intimidated when you first encounter law firm culture. You'll have a more successful experience if you remain adaptable, flexible, and optimistic.

Top Ten Survival Tips for First-Year Students
Working in Law Firms

Here are some of the little things that can make your summer experience run smoother:

1. *Always ask questions.* Even the most trivial things are difficult when you don't know the proper procedure to get something done. NEVER assume **you know** the right way to do things. Asking questions, even about the most trivial things, is viewed favorably.
2. *Make friends with the support staff.* Some support staff members know more about the practice of law than some associates. Figure out who the savvy ones are and become their friends, especially those who have been around forever. They can help you out (and usually want to) more than you realize.
3. *Get along with your peers.* Summer programs have little room for prima

donnas. Get to know your fellow law students, and learn to get along with them. No one has a need for a back-stabber or a one-upper.

4. *Quality over quantity every time.* It is better to produce a few good assignments rather than many mediocre ones. And no one is counting.

5. *Remind attorneys that you are a first-year when necessary.* Sometimes assigning attorneys forget that you are a first-year and have taken only the basic law school courses. This makes tackling some complex assignments almost impossible. If necessary, remind them that you are a first-year rather than get in over your head. It is much easier to stay out of a tough assignment than to get out of something that you had no place in to begin with.

6. *Work hard but take the time to have fun.* Summer programs are meant to be two-dimensional. You must prove that you can do the work, but you also must prove that you can fit in. No one will ever know if you fit in if you are working 100 percent of the time. And life is too short not to have fun at least part of the time. Take the time to get to know the people you are working with, for your benefit as well as theirs. Firms won't hire or invite back students they don't know very well.

7. *Don't burn your bridges.* The law firm community is small, and you can't always predict where you will ultimately end up. If you discover that you don't like the firm where you're working, learn to make the best of it, and if you must leave, always depart on good terms, no matter what your circumstances.

8. *Learn how the politics work in your firm sooner rather than later.* In law firms, like the rest of the corporate world, politics play a leading role. Learn the ropes quickly, as well as how not to become entangled in them. Be aware, but don't get involved.

9. *Be savvy.* If this is your first law firm experience, educate yourself on law firm economics and culture as quickly as possible. Remember that you are not in academia anymore. Listen to the war stories. They can be quite revealing if you are able to separate fact from fiction. At the very least, they can serve as cautionary tales of what not to do.

10. *Be yourself.* Don't try to be someone you are not. This is only a summer job—you don't have to sell your soul.

Some additional advice comes from an article that appeared in a 1989 *ABA Journal.* Attorney Kathy Biehl tells young associates to ground their attitude in reality. "Think of what you're doing as a job . . . and it's okay for jobs to be boring every now and then." I agree. Take the initiative, and learn to expect the unexpected. While your first summer may be just a dress rehearsal, remember, even seasoned actors take dress rehearsals seriously.

WHAT IF YOU DON'T LAND A LAW FIRM JOB FOR THE SUMMER?

What happens if you aren't able to find a law firm job for the summer? Don't worry too much if you find yourself in this same boat as most of your classmates. Although with the continual belt tightening that many firms are still undergoing, this scenario is unlikely to change anytime soon, you still have many options. You'll discover next year that law firms don't turn their noses up at second-year students who have not yet worked in firms.

Some of Your Options

The most important factor from the perspective of law firms is that you did something constructive and creative during your summer. Red flags are raised when employers see students who did nothing educational or productive during the summer. And the universe of "productive" and "educational" jobs is quite large. In other words, lifeguarding for the summer is out, but law school study in Florence is in.

Here are some of your options at this point:

1. *Tie your summer work experience to your previous background or to an area you may have an interest in as a practicing attorney.* For example, one first-year with a strong undergraduate accounting background worked during his first summer as a legal intern at the Treasury Department in Washington, D.C. He worked for free, but the experience set him apart from other candidates as he interviewed during his second year, especially since he was interested in international tax work when he got out of law school. He still views his experience at the Treasury Department as an invaluable component of his legal career.

2. *Go to summer school.* Lighten your workload for your second year when you'll be busy interviewing by taking two or three classes during the summer. Throw yourself into your studies, and improve a disappointing grade point average. Or if you can manage to get the money together, go to Italy or England for the summer—to study, of course.

3. *Work in politics, especially if it's an election year.* While this experience may not be directly transferable to your law school studies, find out early if you have politics in your blood. This can also improve your networking opportunities in the future.

4. *Improve your language skills.* Having multiple language skills is becoming more important in our global economy. Being fluent in another language won't look bad on your resume, either.

5. *Work as an intern in a corporate legal department.* Finding these jobs is

difficult, but students manage to find them all of the time. This is another example of when your networking skills come in handy.

6. *Volunteer.* There are so many agencies that could use the assistance, even part-time, of a bright law student. Work for the Legal Aid Society, the United Way, a hospice, or a soup kitchen. The possibilities are endless. This *always* looks good on a resume.

One very creative student wrote a screenplay over a summer. He decided that this would be his last chance for a while to devote a large chunk of time to his project. Money was in short supply, too. So he put an ad in a New York newspaper, seeking to house-sit a nice home so he wouldn't have to pay rent. He found an executive who owned a home on Long Island who was going to Europe for the summer and needed a responsible person to take care of things while he was gone. The student jumped at the opportunity. He sat in this gorgeous home for almost three months, paying no rent, and wrote his screenplay. You can bet that his story played very well in the fall when he started interviewing with firms.

There are so many things you can do over a summer. And I assure you that law firms are open-minded enough to look at these experiences as useful to a future legal career. Some other first-year summer jobs I've seen over the years include the following: clerking for judges, working for a local government agency, working for a relative's business, real estate development, government agency work, working for an international development organization, and even writing a book or screenplay.

The first-year job market is a tough place to be. Use your golden first-year summer, without the "2L pressure to perform," to your advantage, regardless of whether you end up in a Wall Street firm or on the streets of Venice for the summer. Take a few risks and grasp opportunities that you cannot afford to take during that all-important second-year summer. It's not imperative that you work in a law firm, nor is it expected from the law firm community. Be realistic and creative at the same time. And don't worry if you fail in your attempt to land a coveted big-bucks, big-firm summer position. There will be plenty of time for that, if you decide that is the best path for you to take. Your first-year summer should be an education in itself.

PART TWO

GETTING A SUMMER JOB AS A SECOND-YEAR STUDENT

Hiring people is similar to buying a tie.
You don't buy the tie when you need one.
You buy the tie when you see one and like it.
                    —HENRY GRUNFELD

4

HOW TO MANAGE YOUR SECOND-YEAR JOB SEARCH

"I'm not leaving here until I have an offer!"

The second-year summer internship is probably the most vital stage of the law firm recruiting process. It is extremely difficult to secure an associate position in a major law firm without first being a summer associate. And your chances of getting that job are even better if you are a second-year summer associate. According to the National Association for Law Placement's research on recent fall recruiting seasons, law firms continue to rely on their summer programs as a primary source for new hires. During the fall of 1994, 83 percent of the second-year summer associates received job offers. This statistic is in sharp contrast to the one-third of third-year students who received job offers during the same fall interview period. These facts reinforce that getting a job that second-year summer is much easier than trying to get an offer once you become a third-year student.

But your successful recruiting efforts are the result of sound planning and self-reliance. When second-year students begin the daunting task of looking for a summer job, many are simply overwhelmed by their options, especially when compared to the limited options they had as first-year students. Your search will be much easier if you lay some preliminary groundwork.

ASSESS YOUR GOALS AFTER THE FIRST-YEAR SUMMER

If, after your first-year summer, you don't really know what you want to do during your second-year summer, take a week or two before you return to school for your second year to do some research and to create an action plan. Use the resources of your law school placement office, either at your own school or at one that's convenient. Many law schools have strict rules on reciprocity and don't allow other students to use their resources, so you may have to return to school early to do your research. Even if this cuts into your vacation, in the long run, this will be time well spent.

According to many placement directors, most second-year students bypass the intense career assessment that is critical at this point. Before you try to find a job in a law firm, you should make sure that law firm life is worth the price you will pay for it. I'm advising you from years of experience— make sure you know what you are getting into before you jump in. Sadly, law firms are full of unhappy associates who never should have gone to work in a law firm in the first place.

In addition to personal assessment, seek the advice of career service professionals, who have years of experience advising bright law students on selecting the best work environment for their personality type and future goals. Take advantage of this resource while it is free and at your disposal. This assessment should take place *before* you begin looking for a second-year summer job. Some personality types are well suited for large law firm life; others will fare much better in a smaller work environment. Others are not suited for a career in a law firm at all. Just make sure that you make a well-informed decision about what you want to do, from the beginning.

ESTABLISH A TIMETABLE

As we discussed in Chapter 1, timing is extremely important in your job search. Keep in mind that your own timetable may vary, depending on when you return to school and when your on-campus interviews begin. Use the basic timetable below as a guide. We'll discuss each step in the process.

Second-Year Job Search Timetable

Date	Task
Labor Day	Narrow your geographic focus
Labor Day to mid-September	Narrow your search by area of practice
Labor Day to mid-September	Complete research on law firm culture
Labor Day to mid-September	Establish a job search blueprint
Labor Day to mid-September	Revise resume based on first-year version
Labor Day to mid-September	Begin contacting firms
Early September	Familiarize yourself with the on-campus interview sign-up procedure at your school

NARROW YOUR GEOGRAPHIC FOCUS

Time is of the essence during the fall recruiting season. You'll quickly discover that you will have enough difficulty just managing to attend your classes, schedule on-campus interviews, and complete callbacks to law firms. You simply won't have the time to visit every state in the Union during the fall. You *must* narrow the focus of your job search geographically from the very beginning.

When you start targeting job locations, keep some key facts in mind. The location of the law firm you'll ultimately work for is directly related to your law school's location. According to the NALP'S data on the class of 1994, on a national basis, about 77 percent of graduates accepted their first job in the same region where they attended law school. Eighty-five percent or more went to work in the same region in Florida, South Carolina, Hawaii, Maine, Montana, and Texas. While this may be less significant for regions like New York (which supplied jobs for 2,000 graduates during the same period) and the mid-Atlantic states (where only 67.8 percent of the jobs in the region went to graduates from that region), you should consider these data when planning your job search. New York firms continue to hire such a large number of new lawyers that they tend to seek graduates from all over. The mid-Atlantic region is such a popular place to work (primarily because of the Washington, D.C., market) that it tends to attract candidates from all over the country. This is also the most competitive market in the country for new legal talent. If you attend law school in Southern California, it is unlikely, but not impossible, that you'll be able to secure a position in Pennsylvania without previous connections there. So be realistic about your chances when considering various job locations.

Consider the Geographic Demand for Jobs

Be aware of the current geographic demand for law firm jobs before you begin your job search. For example, the San Francisco and Washington, D.C., markets have been extremely popular in recent years, thus making them extremely competitive. If you are a mediocre student, it may be extremely difficult for you to break into these markets. Every year there are "hot" cities where law students want to work. Be realistic about your chances of breaking into these markets from the beginning. Your placement director can realistically guide you through this maze. He or she is well aware of the current demand to work in certain cities and can bring you back down to earth if necessary. Just stay grounded in reality at all times. Select areas that you realistically have a chance of getting into.

Compare the Cost of Living and Salaries
in Different Markets

Before you begin your job search, you must also consider what it costs to live in an area and whether law firm salaries are high enough to cover your expenses. Don't assume that there is always a positive correlation between law firm salaries and the cost of living in an area. More often than not, your salary will be more than enough to meet your expenses, but there are certain areas where, surprisingly, you may end up living in the red.

For example, for the class of 1994, the average law firm salary in Baltimore was $35,000, according to NALP's research. Many students can't afford to live in Baltimore on $35,000 if they have significant student loan debt. The salaries in San Francisco tend to be lower than in Washington, D.C., for example, even though the cost of housing in San Francisco is much higher. And salaries that may seem low in some areas, such as the Southeast, may actually buy you more, since the cost of living in those areas is so much lower than in other areas of the country.

There are numerous places you can look for this type of economic data. Your placement office has NALP's data on salaries in different parts of the country. That's a great place to begin. Once you have that in hand, here's what you'll need to do to sort out information on the cost of living in the markets you're interested in:

1. Contact local chambers of commerce or trade organizations. They usually have up-to-date statistics on the cost of living in their areas.
2. Refer to the *Statistical Abstract,* which is published annually by the Commerce Department. Your local library should have recent copies.

3. Call local law schools, and ask for information about their area. Who knows better about what it costs to live in an area than those who live there?

Don't Follow the Herd

Beware of the "herd mentality" common to second-year law students. Repeatedly, placement directors report that students are led by their peers, regardless of what they really want. Just because your *Law Review* editors are going to New York does not mean that you also have to work there. As one very experienced placement director advised, "Students need to understand who they are and what they want, regardless of what their friends or family want them to do." This is too big a decision to make based on what your best friend is doing. You are the one who has to decide where you'll be the happiest working.

NARROW YOUR SEARCH BY AREA OF PRACTICE

Once you've narrowed your search by location, the next step is to consider areas of practice. After completing one year of law school, you're probably not sure what areas of the law interest you. It's not absolutely necessary to know what practice area you want to work in at this time. But it is necessary to educate yourself on firm specialties by understanding which firms practice in specific areas of the law. The full-service law firm is disappearing. Many firms have specific areas of expertise or at least work in a few areas. You'll at least know some areas that you don't want to work in. You can start by eliminating those firms that practice in these areas. And nothing turns off firms more than students who haven't done their homework. Placement directors report that students rarely pay attention to the internal demographics of law firms, and I can certainly vouch for that.

Where to Look for Information

You have many research options as you try to decipher which firms do what. Bear in mind, it's much easier to find information on large firms than small ones.

1. You can electronically sort through firms identifying areas of practice via Westlaw or LEXIS/NEXIS. The use of these databases is free to law students. Jane Thieberger, Assistant Dean, Career Counseling and Place-

ment at New York University, has written a helpful guide for online job searchers, *LEXIS/NEXIS Job Searching in an Electronic Age*, available from Mead Data Central. This guide can help you navigate through the abundance of information available through LEXIS/NEXIS—from listings of judges to information on job locations.

2. Refer to NALP's *Directory of Law Firms,* which can be found in your placement office. This annual directory publishes the NALP forms (which include "need to know" statistical information on member firms). Included for each firm is a list of their major practice areas, including the number of attorneys working in each area.

3. Use the information, gathered from former summer associates, about specific law firms in your placement office. This is an invaluable source of information, which placement directors report is rarely used.

4. Refer to *The Insider's Guide to Law Firms*. This book was started by several Harvard law students a few years ago and is published each year. It describes the areas of practice of firms in major U.S. cities. Your placement office may have a copy, or it can be purchased in paperback at large bookstores.

How to Select the Firms That Practice in
Your Areas of Interest

Students often research firms to determine which ones practice in the areas that interest them but still fall short of their goal of finding employment. Just because a firm has attorneys who practice in a specific area doesn't mean that they'll be hiring for that area.

If a firm with sixty-five attorneys lists an intellectual property practice on its NALP form or in its firm brochure, but only two attorneys work in that area, chances are the firm won't hire for that area every year. If, on the other hand, half the firm practices labor law, then you can assume that labor will be an area in which hiring will take place in any given year. If you want to be sure, call the firm and ask in which areas it anticipates hiring for that year. Contact the recruiting office, the office administrator, or the hiring partner.

If you are unsure what you want to do, don't consider a firm that practices in only a few areas—trade, tax, and corporate law, for example—unless you are sure you could be happy working in at least one of those areas. You can save yourself a lot of time in the long run if you do a little research on the front end.

Usually, small firms don't require associates to specialize as the larger ones tend to do. If you take this route, make sure that you can be happy as a generalist, at least for a while. And you may find that your choice of geographic location will dictate firm size and specialty. For example, if you want to do project finance work, you will more than likely end up in New York. High-tech computer work may lead you to the Palo Alto/San Francisco area. Maritime law may pull you toward New Orleans or Baltimore. Small, rural locations rarely need specialists but require attorneys who can wear many hats (and want to). Keep also in mind, as we discussed earlier in this chapter, your current law school location. If you are at a small Texas law school and have your heart set on doing high-level international trade work, which is most abundant in major markets like New York and Washington, you may have an extremely tough time getting a job. Make sure you keep all the pieces to the puzzle in the back of your mind during this process.

RESEARCHING LAW FIRM CULTURE

Probably the most difficult part of the recruiting process is deciphering law firm culture. Every firm, large or small, has its own unique culture. If you don't like the environment and the people, then no matter how good the work is or how high the salary, you may find yourself very unhappy. As Chief Justice William Rehnquist stated at graduation ceremonies at Catholic University's Columbus School of Law, "Don't forget that in choosing a job you're very likely choosing a lifestyle." But how do you decode law firm culture, and when should you begin this process?

Figuring out "what makes a firm tick" is a subjective process, and you should start gathering intelligence as early as possible. As mentioned earlier, to understand what you're looking for, personal career assessment must take place in the very beginning. If you don't know what makes your clock tick, then you won't be able to determine what firm attributes are important to you. The adage "Know thyself" is critical. You'll hear me say this more than once in this book.

Where to Look for Information

There are various places you can go for information about law firm culture, but keep in mind throughout this process that you should let your intuition be your guide. And remember that no source is going to be 100 percent reliable, since much of the information you'll receive is merely someone else's *perception*. Here are some sources of information that can help you get a feel for a large firm's culture:

1. As mentioned earlier in this chapter, most placement offices keep comments on file about firms from former summer associates. This is an invaluable source of information, which, as mentioned earlier, is used infrequently.

2. *The Insider's Guide to Law Firms*, also mentioned earlier, is another excellent source. It contains up-to-date "off the record" data on many major firms in the major metropolitan areas. While this book may prove helpful, keep in mind that the information it contains is based solely on the *perception* of the students who worked in the various firms.

3. The *American Lawyer* publishes a biannual report in its October issue on summer programs. They actually rank the programs in larger cities, after tabulating questionnaires completed by actual summer associates. At the very least, this publication will tell you who runs the best and worst summer programs according to a wide sampling of responses.

Gathering data on small-firm culture is more difficult. Contact local bar associations for legal directories. Using these directories, call other attorneys in the area, and ask for references. Read the local paper to see who is making the legal news. Ask judges and public prosecutors for recommendations. Put your networking skills to work.

But as you gather intelligence from your friends and from other sources, keep their experiences in perspective. Perception is not always reality. Just because Bill Smith did not like Cain & Abel does not mean that you will have the same experience. But if your best friend had a bad summer at a firm because women who had families were treated as second-class citizens and that's an issue for you, then you should give her advice serious consideration. Much of the intuitive data will be gathered as you go through the actual recruiting process. A firm's environment speaks in volume.

ESTABLISH A JOB SEARCH BLUEPRINT

Now that you have made the necessary internal and external assessments about your wants and needs, the real part of your journey begins. But as you go through the recruiting process, it's helpful to have a blueprint to refer back to, just to ensure that you don't lose sight of where you're going. Below is a sample second-year blueprint for our fictitious law student, Emma Smith, for you to use as a guide. I encourage you to create your own blueprint before you begin your journey through the second-year recruiting jungle.

Notice that Emma has narrowed her focus geographically, with backup locations, and has a general idea of the size of firm she wants to work for. Her area of practice interest is a little fuzzy, but she has eliminated some areas, and she has selected a few cultural attributes that are important to her. While she may not end up working in a firm with all of these characteristics, this exercise will help her narrow her focus and guide her as she is bombarded with choices.

Emma Smith—Blueprint for Recruiting

Goal	To secure a summer associate/associate position in a law firm
Primary location	Atlanta, Georgia
	Charlotte, North Carolina
Backup location	Memphis, Tennessee
	Nashville, Tennessee
Ideal firm size	150 attorneys or less
Branch or main office	Open to either
Areas of practice	General practice firm
	Possible interest in corporate/banking
Areas **not** interested in	Litigation
	Intellectual property
	Tax planning
	Bankruptcy
	ERISA
Culture/firm attributes	Entrepreneurial
	Open to various religious and social groups
	Community oriented

THE SECOND-YEAR RESUME

Now that you have narrowed your focus by location, type of law firm, and practice area, your next step is create a resume that will aid you in getting the law firm job you want. Remember the primary rule of marketing as you do this—if you haven't targeted your market, putting together your resume will be extremely difficult. Remember, a resume is a marketing tool, and any marketing expert will tell you that it's much easier to sell your product if you know who your market is.

Work from Your First-Year Resume

There should be few significant differences between your first-year and second-year resumes. For a comparison exercise, we'll review the first-year resume of Emma Smith, found on page 15, and we'll make the necessary changes to market Emma as a second-year student. In addition, we'll use the blueprint we developed for Emma earlier in this chapter to help direct her job search. Her market is already targeted and focused, which will help us to determine what to incorporate and focus on in her resume.

Like the first-year resume, the second-year version should be one page in length unless you have significant work experience. The format should be similar to that used in the first-year resume. As in the first-year version, educational history should be listed first, followed by work experience, language and computer skills, and personal interests. References should not be listed on the resume. Refer to the list under First-Year Resume Do's and Don'ts in Chapter 2 for guidance. These rules also apply to the second-year resume.

How to Shape Your Second-Year Resume
Using Your First-Year Version

To demonstrate how your second-year resume should build on your first-year version, let's revisit Emma. Review her job search blueprint earlier in this chapter. Emma's goal is to work in a law firm in Atlanta. Her second-choice cities are Charlotte, Memphis, and Nashville. She's interested in working in a 150-attorney firm (or less), which is large for these markets. She's not completely focused on her practice area but has a possible interest in corporate or banking work. Areas of law that she is not interested in include ERISA, bankruptcy, tax planning, intellectual property, and litigation. Emma is committed to community service work and is interested in a firm that embraces that concept. She is somewhat entrepreneurial and is open-minded about working with a diverse group of people.

These facts and ideas will help shape Emma's resume and her cover letter. Let's refer to her second-year resume below and see how we do this.

1. *Education and grades:* You'll notice that I haven't included her law school grades. You usually don't see grades on resumes from top tier schools such as Harvard simply because, since it's so difficult to get into the school, once you're there, grades aren't as important as at some other schools. As a general rule, if your grades are good (an average above 3.0 on a 4.0 scale), include them. If the grading scale at your school is unusual, educate your audience by indicating where you fall within your class. Also, indicate if you are estimating your class rank. Columbia and SUNY-Buffalo, for example, have unique grading systems that most resume readers are not familiar with.

   I've included Emma's high school education on her resume because she was class valedictorian and because the school ties her to the South, where she wants to work. Her undergraduate school also binds her geographically, but those factors alone may not be enough to land her a job in the South.

2. *First-year summer employment:* I've listed Emma's first-year summer employment, briefly explaining what she did while at the firm. Make it clear, if the firm is relatively unknown, that you worked for a law firm.

Second-Year Resume

Emma L. Smith
1588 Beacon Street, Apt. 8
Boston, MA 02142
617-352-5666
e-mail: emmalsmith@aol.com

Education

HARVARD LAW SCHOOL, J.D., expected 1997
Honors: First Place, Williams Contract Negotiation Competition
Activities: Big Brothers/Sisters Program, Resident Assistant
EMORY UNIVERSITY, Atlanta, Ga., B.A., History, 1994
Summa cum laude, Phi Beta Kappa
Varsity Tennis Team, Departmental Thesis Award
Personally financed 75% of college expenses with part-time and summer
jobs.
Salem Academy, Winston-Salem, N.C.
Graduated 1990, Valedictorian

Experience

Albert, Flint & Moore

Summer
1995

Charlotte, N.C.
Summer Associate (invitation to return during 2L summer)
Assisted in drafting general correspondence and research for corporate
clients and related real estate matters. Worked closely with senior partner in
civil litigation matter for major Louisiana shipping company. Participated
in strategy sessions.

U.S. China Forum

Summer
1994

Washington, D.C.
Research Assistant
Organized and administered Chinese educational programs for visiting
dignitaries.
Performed related research and translated documents from Chinese to
English.

Wellington Smith, C.P.A.

Summers
1990–1993

Charlotte, N.C.
Accounting Assistant
Worked in family-owned accounting practice. Performed general office
functions, set up new computer system, trained personnel, negotiated contracts with vendors.

Languages   Fluent in Mandarin Chinese and French

Interests/Skills

Familiar with WordPerfect, Excel, and Lotus. Interests include tennis, community service, and Chinese art. Classical pianist.

Be sure that your audience understands what type of company you worked for, no matter what you did. If you received an offer to work there or to return during your second summer, also include that information.

3. *"Other experience"*: I've deleted the "Other Experience" information from Emma's second-year resume. If you need this information for "filler" to make your resume longer, leave it. Otherwise, delete it.

As with your first-year resume, the second-year version should be clear, concise, and easy to read, and there should be enough white space to make it easy to pick up the main focus points—educational background and work history. Your resume should be interesting to the reader—it should make the reader want to meet you and talk to you in person. The same rules we discussed in Chapter 2 on preparing a resume apply again. Refer to that section for a refresher if you need to.

THE COVER LETTER

The second-year cover letter should be similar to your first-year version, with a few minor differences. Refer again to the basic guidelines on preparing cover letters in Chapter 2. The primary difference is that the second-year letter should be more targeted to your particular audience, which you have already thoroughly researched. If you've done your homework, composition will be much easier. Refer to the sample second-year cover letter on page 55.

Your cover letter should highlight the fact that you're interested in working in a certain geographic area for a particular type of law firm. It will probably be necessary to create a different letter for each audience. So if you have narrowed your focus, you realize how time-consuming this process can be.

In Emma's case, she'll compose a different letter for each of the cities she is interested in, explaining why she has selected those cities and law firms, assuming that the firms in those markets are approximately the same size and have similar practices. Always date your letter, and sign it in blue ink. Blue ink demonstrates that you haven't photocopied your cover letters and mailed them.

CONTACTING FIRMS

Once you identify your target market and compose your resume and cover letter, you're ready to proceed with the next part of your blueprint—contacting the firms you've determined you're interested in. Contact the firms on

Second-Year Cover Letter

1588 Beacon Street, Apt. 8
Boston, MA 02142
617-352-5666

September 6, 1995

Ms. Mary S. Jenkins
Director of Recruiting
Jones, Smith & Butters
299 West Market Street
Suite 800
Atlanta, GA 30309

Dear Ms. Jenkins:

I am a second-year law student at Harvard, originally from Atlanta, and am interested in working in Atlanta next summer. My resume is attached for your review and consideration.

Sometime in October, I plan to return to Atlanta for interviews and would like to talk with members of your firm about a possible summer clerkship. I noticed that your firm was not scheduled to visit Harvard this fall. I have a strong law and undergraduate record and am interested in working for a civic-minded firm with a substantial general practice. I also have a possible interest in general corporate work.

Once my plans to return to Atlanta are concrete, I will call you so that we might be able to set up a mutually convenient time for an interview. If you have any questions, please contact me directly at 617-352-5666. Thank you, in advance, for your time and consideration, and I look forward to talking with you.

Sincerely,

Emma L. Smith

your list from Labor Day to mid-September. You want to wait until the summer programs end, but you want to get your resume in before the on-campus interview process gets under way. If your school holds interviews prior to Labor Day, get your resume in by mid-August.

Firms Interviewing On-Campus at Your School

Determine which firms are coming to your campus that you want to interview with, and sign up to talk with them through your placement office. The procedure will vary at every school, so be familiar with yours *before* interviews get under way. You may want to consider contacting these firms prior to their visit, giving them a "heads up" that you're particularly interested in interviewing with them, especially if prescreening is allowed. Prescreening means that the firm can select the students it wants to interview. Some firms pay attention to these resumes, while others will not. Much depends on how your on-campus interview selection process works. If your school has a lottery system, you will need to contact the firms you want to see if you were not selected through the lottery. If a firm is coming to your campus and you also mail your resume, do not become a pest. Mail your resume, and wait to see if you get an interview.

Firms That Are Not Coming to Your School

Make a list of the firms you are interested in that are not coming to your school to interview. Mail your resume to these firms, and then follow up with a telephone call. Make a list and keep track of your progress, indicating the date your resume was mailed, the date of your follow-up phone call, and the result.

Those firms that are not visiting your school should be contacted early in the fall, around Labor Day. Follow up with these firms approximately two weeks later. Follow the rules and procedures we established in Chapter 2. The same rules apply for mailing second-year resumes.

Use the Correct Etiquette When Following Up with Firms

As we discussed in Chapter 2, it's extremely important that you follow up with the firms to which you mail your resume. Often resumes fall between the cracks or get lost in the mail. You want to make sure that the resume arrived safe and sound. But there is an etiquette involved in corresponding with firms, which you should follow during this chaotic time of year:

1. *Be sympathetic to recruiting coordinators.* You should realize how over-worked recruiting professionals are during the fall. No amount of organi-

zational skill can compensate for the workload. When you call a recruiting coordinator and say "Hello, I'm Bill Smith from South Texas. Did you receive the resume I mailed last Monday?" it drives them crazy. Remember, your resume may be one of **hundreds** received during that week alone. Some firms have large recruiting staffs and computerized databases for recruiting, but many don't. In small firms, reading resumes often falls into the lap of an overworked partner or his or her assistant.

2. *Allow ample time for your resume to arrive and don't be a pest.* Then, if applicable, indicate that you're planning to be in town for interviews and want to know if there's interest in talking with you. If necessary, give a brief synopsis of your background. If no decision has been made regarding your candidacy, ask when such decisions will be made. It is not unreasonable to ask for a timetable.

3. *Be respectful of whatever response you receive.* When you call, some recruiting professionals will tell you that they are full, that they only interview on-campus, that they will talk to you only if you pay your way, that they will pull your resume and get back to you at a later date, or that they are simply not interested in you. Be respectful of the message sent, and realize that, for many firms, hiring students is often a numbers game.

4. *Call early, before 9:00 A.M., or at the end of the day, after 4:00 P.M.* Often, during the day, recruiting professionals are away from their offices or on the telephone. These are the best times to get hold of them.

5. *Learn to take rejection well.* You'll probably receive thirty times as many "no's" as you will "yes's" during the recruiting process. Most students do not follow up on mailed resumes because of the fear of rejection. Even the best and the brightest students get turned down during this process.

Planning ahead and establishing a general idea of what you are looking for in a firm will put you miles ahead of your peers. If you have an idea of what you're looking for in a firm and know which firms you realistically have a shot at, your efforts will not go unnoticed. You may even have time to attend a class or two during this hectic time period.

5

LAYING THE GROUND-WORK BEFORE AN ON-CAMPUS INTERVIEW

"Have I hit all the hot-button subjects?"

The on-campus interview is a critical component of the fall recruiting season. Your chances of securing second-year summer employment will be much greater if you successfully tame this wild animal. But students are usually not privy to some of the decisions that are made inside law firms prior to their on-campus visits, such as how schools are chosen, why firms stop going to some schools, how firms rate job fairs and consortia and why they don't attend many of them, and how students are selected for callbacks after on-campus interviews. These issues may seem irrelevant, but they are crucial to your success.

WHY FIRMS VISIT SOME SCHOOLS AND NOT OTHERS

Understanding why firms visit only certain schools is beneficial if your school doesn't attract the firms you're interested in interviewing with. If you understand what factors keep firms from visiting your campus, you may learn not to waste your time with that firm, or you may be able to overcome the obstacles that keep firms from your campus in the first place. Let's face it, if you consider that there are 180 American Bar Association–approved law schools and the median number of campus visits per firm was nine in 1994, you quickly see that many schools don't attract a large number of firms to their campuses. Also, keep in mind that many small firms don't go on-campus at all. So what factors are important to firms when they decide which schools to visit each fall?

The Geographic Pull

Statistics from the National Association for Law Placement tell us that firms routinely visit schools that are geographically convenient to them. For example, many Washington, D.C., firms visit the abundant number of local law schools and therefore don't have to venture outside of the Washington metropolitan area to fill their positions. The same scenario exists in the Boston and San Francisco area markets.

The NALP form will tell you which schools a firm visits each year. As you review each form, the geographic pull quickly becomes apparent. It's unrealistic to assume that the New York office of Brown & Wood is going to make an on-campus visit to the South Texas School of Law unless someone has a connection to South Texas. But also realize that firms make these decisions independently, and what works for one firm may not necessarily work for another.

This obviously makes it more difficult for students in more remote areas to find employment. Students at the University of Maine School of Law, for example, have an easier shot at jobs in Maine than in Dallas, Texas. Once you enroll at a school, there isn't much you can do about the geographic pull. Just be realistic about your opportunities when you begin your job search.

Repeat Performances

Firms tend to select schools that have proven, over the years, to offer them an abundant number of summer associates. If a firm has successful recruiting trips at a school, year after year, it is likely to continue using that school as a hiring source. And in this age of economic belt tightening, firms are eliminating all but those schools that supply them repeatedly with summer associates who accept their offers and ultimately become good associates.

A Firm May Have Alumnae Connections

Some schools are chosen because influential partners or a large number of attorneys in the firm attended them. For example, one medium-sized firm in the Southeast employs a large number of attorneys from Yale. Year after year, the firm interviews and hires from Yale, and no other firm in the area attracts as many Yale students.

Also, if a partner is a member of the board of visitors at a school or has a son or daughter attending that school, you sometimes find the firm interviewing on-campus. But economic belt tightening has slowed this practice.

Firms Like to Visit the "Top" Schools

Law firms are snobs. They like to hire the best and the brightest from the top law schools. Many people will argue that the students at less prestigious schools are equally as bright as those in the Ivy League, but lawyers want to fill their offices with their perception of the "best and the brightest," whatever that is. As snobbish and narrow-minded as it may seem, law firms, especially the large ones, will continue to recruit from the top schools in this country no matter what.

WHY FIRMS QUIT GOING TO SOME SCHOOLS

Understanding why firms quit going to certain schools is equally important. Knowing these "whys" may again help you overcome the obstacles that keep you from getting the interviews with the firms you want. But the process may take some work on your part. For example, if Smith & Jones quit coming to your law school because they were having trouble attracting the students they wanted to hire, you may be able to get an interview if you can convince them that you're genuinely interested in the firm. As mentioned in Chapter 1, firms are hiring fewer students, which means less on-campus interviewing. You have to play smarter and be more realistic about your odds during the on-campus interview process.

Cutting Back to Save Money

Law firms are watching the bottom line like hawks. If a school doesn't deliver after a few years, firms divert their resources to other schools. Look at the statistics in your placement office. If a particular firm's batting average is low, you may not see that firm the following year on-campus.

Some firms are simply cutting back, despite their success ratios at particular schools. One well-known East Coast boutique firm is now going to fewer schools every year but is making a stronger effort at a smaller number of schools. The firm's reasoning behind this, according to the recruiting coordinator, is that "those students who really know what they want find us."

This firm, while interviewing less on-campus, considers most students who write in who are in the top 5 percent of their class.

As mentioned earlier, firms are looking at their numbers, and if they aren't successful at a school, they're going somewhere else. Some schools act as "feeders" to certain law firms, supplying those firms with large numbers of students. When the "feeding" stops, the firms are packing up and taking their goods elsewhere.

Firms are Creating Their Own Strategic Plans

Firms often include recruiting in their strategic planning efforts. Sometimes firms have their own ideas about recruiting, and they experiment. One well-known large firm decided to visit a larger number of schools, hiring almost exclusively from that pool, eliminating interviews from mailed unsolicited resumes. It was more economical for the firm to select candidates using this method, rather than bringing in large numbers of candidates who simply looked good on paper, taking hundreds of hours of expensive billable attorney time. This plan worked very well for the firm, and it achieved its long-range recruiting goals.

WHY JOB FAIRS AND CONSORTIA ARE VALUABLE RECRUITING TOOLS

Job fairs provide an economical alternative to the on-campus interview for both students and firms. You come to one location and interview with multiple firms, usually in one day. Often, there is a specific group sponsoring the job fair. For example, there is a Texas in Washington Job Fair for students who attend school in Texas who want to work in the nation's capital. Minority groups also sponsor job fairs, and many schools host job fairs in large cities for their students, often with other area schools. Job fairs also bring together students who are interested in one area of law—intellectual property or litigation, for example.

It makes good sense to meet with firms at job fairs. In a day's time, you may be able to meet with ten or fifteen firms. And the purpose of job fairs, from a firm's perspective, is a little different from that of an on-campus interview. Yes, firms come to job fairs with the intention of hiring students, but they also view job fairs as a marketing tool. You also go to be seen and get your name out to a wider audience.

Firms are often less stringent in their academic requirements at job fairs because the structure is less rigid, and students tend to get in to see firms they may not be qualified for "on paper." I can think of many times that I interviewed students at job fairs whom I would never have seen on-campus, really liked the person, and sometimes ended up hiring. You might mistakenly think that more small firms attend job fairs than large ones. The 240 firms providing data for NALP's fall 1994 survey reported participating in 280 job fairs or consortia. But surprisingly, firms with over 100 attorneys participated in job fairs more often than their smaller counterparts. About half of offices of 100 attorneys or fewer reported no job fair participation compared with 24.3 percent of larger offices. Over one-third of larger offices participated in two or more job fairs.

HOW TO GET YOUR RESUME SELECTED FOR ON-CAMPUS INTERVIEWS

If your school allows firms to prescreen resumes and select the students they wish to interview before coming on-campus, it's helpful to understand how firms make these initial selections so that you'll have a better chance of getting your resume selected. The selection process varies among firms, but most firms establish basic standards, which are usually academic, that most candidates must meet.

Students have little control once the resumes are in the hands of the law firms. Your job is to deliver a clear, concise resume to the firm, following the firm's basic criteria. This means paying attention to the academic guidelines as well as knowing the areas of law in which the firm practices. It is much more difficult to predict the more intangible features firms may look for. Don't try to second-guess what these things might be. Simply do your homework ahead of time, and follow the basic guidelines already established.

How the Resume Review Process Works

1. *Resumes are reviewed and sorted.* Resumes are typically mailed to the recruiting coordinator in large firms and to the hiring partner or administrator in smaller firms. This individual typically reviews the resumes first. This is a daunting task if the firm receives a huge number of resumes. It's not unusual to receive 75 resumes from a class of 350 students. The recruiting coordinator will often take the first cut, eliminating resumes that do not fall into the same galaxy as the initial criteria set by the firm. He or she will then sort the resumes, putting aside those that fall short academically but are otherwise acceptable and those that fit academically and appear to have suitable backgrounds for the firm.

2. *Some resumes are given a chance even if they don't fit the firm's set criteria.* Because the numbers are often so huge, firms are forced to establish general academic criteria when selecting resumes, although this process is not always absolute. For example, a firm with a strong tax practice might consider the resume of a student with a significant accounting background and related work experience even if the student's grades are slightly lower than their target level. But if a firm says it wants to see resumes from the top quarter of the class and this student is in the bottom quarter, it's unlikely that this student will make the cut. Rules are bent but usually not broken.

3. *Firms look for traits on resumes that may indicate future success at that firm.* They look for other facts on resumes outside of grades, educational history, and work experience. For instance, at Baker & McKenzie, we looked for students with international backgrounds or entrepreneurial promise. One student was hired because the firm liked the entrepreneurial spirit demonstrated by his college-based business. A litigation firm might look for aggressive personality traits that may indicate a potential for trial work—debate team experience, for example. Some firms may look for community service experience if that trait is a strong indicator of future success there. The weight of this factor will vary with each firm. Hiring exclusively on this type of criterion is the exception and not the norm.

4. *"Inside information" on candidates is sometimes gathered.* Occasionally, attorneys contact professors for inside information on candidates if there is a personal connection. If a promising resume comes through and an attorney knows the student's contracts professor, the attorney may take the liberty of calling that professor for more information on the student. Also, professors are sometimes contacted to help make the call on borderline candidates.

5. *An alumnus may make a final review of the resumes to ensure that nothing is missed.* Sometimes, an attorney in the firm who attended the school will review the resumes. For example, a student may have a good record with one low grade from a professor who has a reputation for being extremely tough. Exceptions are made with complete information in many instances.

6. *The final cut is often handled by the hiring partner, hiring committee, recruiting coordinator, or a combination of the three.* Sometimes, however, this job falls to the attorneys designated to go on-campus to that school.

Who Does the Interviewing

Firms often send hiring committee members to interview students on-campus. This makes sense, as committee members are usually interested in recruiting, knowledgeable about the process in their firm, and often trained in interviewing. If committee members aren't available, alumnae often go. And don't be surprised if you have a last-minute fill-in at an interview. Client demands sometimes force attorneys to change their plans at the last minute. Some firms are now sending two interviewers on-campus. Interviewing is so exhausting that two people instead of one make the day go much easier. And if a firm has a very large practice area, you'll often find someone who is knowledgeable about that area on-campus. Another trend is sending recruiting coordinators on-campus, since they generally run the program anyway.

HELPFUL HINTS TO PREPARE FOR THE ON-CAMPUS INTERVIEW

In recruiting, preparation is nine-tenths of the law. As you prepare for on-campus interviews, keep the following tips in mind:

1. *Pay attention to deadlines.* Nothing irritates a firm more than receiving a resume after the on-campus interview. In most cases, if you missed the boat, it won't come back to pick you up.
2. *Accept your fate.* If you are denied an interview, accept it and move on. Firms are unlikely to reverse initial decisions when prescreening is allowed, especially for candidates who don't meet their hiring criteria.
3. *Pay attention to hiring criteria.* If a firm wants to interview students in the top third of the class and you are in the bottom third, don't waste your time or theirs. "If they could only meet me" just isn't enough. Be realistic about your chances.
4. *Listen to your placement director.* If you find yourself with no interviews, talk to your placement director for guidance and direction. He or she is a pro and can help you. But listen to what you are told and follow the advice you're given so that you end up with some choices at the end of the fall.
5. *Don't rely exclusively on the on-campus interview process.* A common, regretted mistake is taking the easy way out and relying almost exclusively on on-campus interviews. Many students fail to get jobs using this vehicle. Make sure you have other options available to you. Put the burden on yourself to have a contingency plan in case your on-campus plans

don't go as expected. Look to positions in the government sector, non-profit organizations, and the corporate world.

6. *Plan, persevere, and don't procrastinate.* Even the best laid plans can go awry, but you won't be successful if you wait until the last minute to research firms, create a resume, and decide with whom you really want to interview. Time is of the essence in the recruiting process.

6

MASTERING ON-CAMPUS INTERVIEWS

"I'll just be a sec . . ."

At best, the on-campus interview process is a frenzied time period that former law students recall with about as much fondness as having teeth pulled. Tackling a full course load with days full of twenty- and thirty-minute interviews—which are often out of your control to schedule—is exhausting, no matter what your mental and physical capacity. But I'm going to give you some advice that should help you find your way through this maze. I've seen too many students make the same mistakes over and over again. I'm going to make sure you don't follow in those footsteps.

UNDERSTAND THE INTERVIEW PROCESS AT YOUR SCHOOL

The on-campus interview process varies tremendously among schools. Many schools allow employers to prescreen resumes, while others have instituted some form of lottery system in which the actual selection process is left to chance. There is great debate among law firms and career service professionals as to which system provides employers with the students they want to hire and vice versa, in the most equitable manner. You must work under the rules established at your school, whatever method has been devised. Most schools offer an orientation to the placement office that clearly outlines their rules and regulations. Make sure you attend this program. Some schools have elaborate programs where the number of employers far outweighs the student population, while others struggle to attract even a small number of firms. Too many students make the mistake of not thoroughly understanding how their own school's process works until it's too late. *Don't let this happen to you.* Associates and recent law school graduates repeatedly tell me that they relied entirely too much on the on-campus recruiting process and their career services office. If you don't possess stellar credentials, use the on-campus vehicle, but don't depend on it entirely, or you may find yourself without a summer clerkship in a law firm.

BASIC RULES FOR SUCCESSFUL INTERVIEWS

Interviewing is an acquired art. If you have limited interviewing experience, practice until you are blue in the face. Rehearsing your role in an interview can make the difference between getting a callback or being canned. Some placement offices have the resources to videotape mock interviews for their students, and others offer intensive interview training courses. The following are some routine interview guidelines that will help lead you through the process successfully. While some of these suggestions may sound rudimentary or may be construed as common sense, it is surprising how sometimes even the brightest students arrive ill-prepared for interviews.

1. *Get plenty of rest.* Never underestimate the amount of energy it takes to interview. Get plenty of sleep and eat right in the days leading up to the interview.
2. *Look and act the part.* Students should present themselves in the best manner possible without making a fashion statement. This means following the same wardrobe guidelines we discussed in Chapter 3. You should look and act as though you were going to meet an important dignitary for a business lunch. Wear a nice, pressed suit, and make sure your hair is neatly combed. Wear minimal jewelry. Don't leave your manners at home. Use formal names (i.e., "Mr." and "Ms.") until directed otherwise. Don't sit until everyone else in the room has been seated. Sit up straight, look other people straight in the eyes, and be attentive. If you aren't familiar with formal business etiquette, buy an etiquette book and brush up.
3. *Leave arrogance at home.* Surprisingly, some students come across as arrogant during interviews. Don't assume that just because your credentials are stellar that you'll receive a callback. Many smart, cocky students find themselves with few callbacks because of their attitude.

4. *Do your homework.* Come prepared with at least a few "nontypical" questions even if you don't have time to ask them.

5. *Be courteous.* This means thanking the interviewers for their time, waiting patiently if necessary, and standing up to meet others who enter the room. Use surnames unless instructed otherwise. Formality is the norm throughout the interview process unless the interviewers set a different tone.

6. *Use your best judgment at all times.* If the interviewer is rude or demonstrates unethical conduct during the interview, keep your cool and talk to your placement director immediately following the interview. Let the interview take its normal twenty- or thirty-minute course, and then go through the proper channels to remedy the situation. Just because someone else does not follow the rules doesn't mean that you don't have to.

7. *Strategically select interview times.* If possible, avoid the first interview slot, the slots immediately before and after lunch, and the last slots of the day. Pick times midmorning and midafternoon, when interviewers tend to be more alert and not looking at their watches, waiting for meal breaks, or wanting to go home. This can make a tremendous difference.

8. *Act assertive, not aggressive.* Act as though you are confident even if you're not. This begins with your knock at the door when your interview time arrives, even if another student is in the room. Shake hands firmly with the interviewer, then introduce yourself, and sit down once the interviewer is seated.

9. *Bring your resume with you.* Always bring a few copies of your resume to the interview just in case the interviewer left it at home or didn't receive one from the placement office. If you have a current transcript, bring that as well.

10. *Maintain eye contact with the interviewer.* Interviewers hate it when students fail to look them straight in the eyes during an interview. Lack of eye contact indicates lack of self-confidence or interest in the firm.

11. *Don't be overzealous.* You should be enthusiastic, but do not overdo it. A student with too much enthusiasm is annoying and turns off an interviewer quickly. You want to make sure that you don't come off as patronizing. Interviewers see through that quickly.

12. *Be cognizant of your body language.* No one expects you to become a professional interviewer overnight, but pay attention to the signals your body language sends to the interviewer. Don't cross your arms. Sit erect, facing the interviewer at all times. Make sure you don't play with your hair. The interviewer should have the undivided attention of your body as well as your brain.

13. *Be businesslike.* Interviewers are turned off by students who are too casual. Be relaxed, but don't overdo it. Sit erect in your chair. If you're wearing a skirt, make sure your legs are crossed.
14. *Enjoy the time, and have fun.* While most interviews are not always fun, you can learn from the experience, meet some very interesting people, and learn a lot about yourself.

THE IDEAL INTERVIEW

There is a logical sequence to an on-campus interview, although not every interviewer follows it. While you, as a student, aren't supposed to control the flow of the interview, it's helpful to understand how a properly conducted interview should flow.

The Purpose

The purpose of the on-campus interview is for the firm to determine if you, the student, are someone they want to bring back to the firm, at a future date, for further interviews. You are there to determine if you are interested enough in the firm to warrant further exploration through a callback interview if you are, in fact, invited back. At this stage, the purpose is not to ascertain if you ultimately want to work at that firm. Consider an on-campus interview as an initial screening process, nothing more.

The Process

Broken down into segments, a twenty-minute on-campus interview should ideally function as follows:

1. *Initial greeting (three to five minutes):* The interviewer will engage in small talk to set you at ease. You should firmly shake hands, having eye contact. Ask the interviewer if he or she has a copy of your resume, just to make sure.
2. *The meat of the interview (eight to ten minutes):* This is the informational part of the interview. If the interviewer does his or her job correctly, you should do most of the talking, taking cues from the interviewer. Ideally, your resume will have been read prior to the interview. The interviewer should only pick out pieces of your background for discussion or clarification. He or she should talk less than 10 percent of the time. You should be prepared to talk almost completely during this time period. Be totally familiar with your resume, and have a thorough

knowledge of the firm with which you're interviewing. You won't know what questions you'll be asked, so just be yourself and respond in a relaxed, yet confident manner.

3. *Closing (three to five minutes):* You should ask questions during this period if time permits, and when the next student knocks at the door, the interview should be wrapped up. The interviewer will indicate how and when you will hear back from the firm.

Obviously, not all interviews follow this format, and you may leave an interview learning very little about the firm you interviewed with. Attorneys love to talk about themselves and their work, and it's common for a student to leave an interview only with information on the past Sunday's NFL game. Experienced recruiters know better because they don't want to come home knowing little more than what they read on the resumes.

THE LESS THAN IDEAL INTERVIEW

Part of "the art of interviewing" is learning how to sell yourself even under adverse circumstances. There is no doubt that you'll encounter the interviewer who talks only about the movie he just saw, offering zero insight into his law firm, or the one who prefers to discuss politics or the recent wine harvest in Chile. Some of the high-powered law firm representatives, albeit excellent attorneys, are terrible interviewers and, worst case scenario, will make fools of themselves during this process.

Handling a Bad Interview

Should you write off a firm in which you were really interested because the on-campus interviewer was lousy or acted like a jerk? Only you can make that call, but remember that you ultimately choose a firm not because it has savvy interviewers, but because you like the people and its practice. But learn the difference between an inept interviewer and a jerk who crosses the line of normal interview etiquette.

One such episode involved a student who listed "magic tricks" as a hobby on his resume. During an on-campus interview, the interviewing partner wanted to "test" him and actually asked him to perform a magic trick. Another attorney, noting that a student was fluent in French, conducted the entire interview in the language, just to test the student's language capabilities (and to show off his own language skills). Neither interviewer accomplished anything by acting like jerks during the interview process.

When You Screw Up

Students also make mistakes during on-campus interviews, so you, as a rookie interviewee, should also be prepared to fumble. I was interviewing with a partner one year at a law school in New York, and a zealous student came in and expounded for almost five minutes on his sincere interest in our firm's maritime law practice. I kept kicking the partner I was interviewing with under the table, as I was baffled. Our firm had no maritime practice, and I was wondering why the student was even talking to us. The partner finally interrupted the student's dialogue to sadly inform him that our firm worked in many areas but none of them included maritime law. The student was extremely embarrassed, but clearly he had not done his homework, and he left the interview with his tail between his legs. He screwed the interview up and obviously didn't receive a callback. But hopefully, he learned his lesson and did his homework before his next interview. When you make mistakes, and you will, just make sure that you learn from the experience and don't make the same blunder again.

Everyone nervously hears similar stories, such as the unfortunate student who interviewed with his fly down or the one who called the interviewer by the wrong name. These mishaps happen to even the best prepared students. Don't let unfortunate events—big or small —bring your confidence level down below sea level, but do your homework. Rest assured that it is probable that one of these misfortunes could have your name on it. Just learn to take your mistakes in stride.

FOLLOWING UP AFTER ON-CAMPUS INTERVIEWS

Sending thank-you notes to on-campus interviewers can only make you look good—if you do it correctly. Students who want to make a positive first impression should send a brief thank-you note to the interviewer(s) immediately following the interview. You're going to find it difficult to find the time to write these letters so quickly with everything you have going on at this time of year, but make sure you discipline yourself so that it gets done in a timely fashion.

What to Include in Your Note

1. Thank the interviewers for their time, making reference, if possible, to an interesting part of the conversation that took place during the interview. You'll have to keep good notes from your interviews in order to do

this. If you talked about a certain case or area of law, you could make reference to it. This will help jar the interviewer's memory, since twenty students interviewed in a day tend to run together after a while.

2. Handwrite your note, or do it on a computer, just as long as it is neat, legible, and professional in appearance, with no typographical errors. Follow the same guidelines established for first-year students discussed in Chapter 3.

3. Mail the letter no more than three or four days after the interview. You'll get more bang for your buck the quicker the letter is received, even if it sits on an attorney's desk.

4. If you promised to send the firm additional information such as a transcript or writing sample, this is an ideal time to mail these items to the firm.

CALLBACK DECISIONS

There's no need to be in the dark about how firms make their callback decisions after on-campus interviews. Again, understanding how these decisions are made can help you piece the puzzles of law firm recruiting together.

How Firms Make Callback Decisions

Despite what many law students and placement professionals may think, there is no exact science to the method firms use to make callback decisions. Often it's simply a numbers game, especially for the large firms. Firms decide how many students to call back after on-campus interviews using different forecasting techniques. Some firms have years of statistical data to back up how these decisions are made well into the future, and others don't have a clue as to how it was done in the past and simply choose the students they like.

At Baker & McKenzie's Washington office, we could estimate how many offers we needed to make to arrive at a summer program of a certain size. For example, Baker usually brought in about 50 students for interviews to end up with a ten- to twelve-student summer program. These estimates were based on the percentage of offers and acceptances over the previous three to five years. If the firm visited twelve schools, they could figure out approximately how many students they could bring in from each school, keeping in mind whether trips to these schools came early or late in the interview season.

If a firm has an early interview date at a top law school, it is generally accepted that a firm will get a bigger sign-up and see better students. Years of experience have shown me that this is usually the case. If a firm is interviewing during the last week at a school, a firm's pickings are usually not as good, especially at a top school.

Most firms do not have an established number of students they plan to invite back to the firm from each school. I have been on some interview trips where no one was called back and on others where ten of twenty students were called back to a firm. Some firms give the on-campus interviewers complete control over the callback selection process. Others have a hiring committee member or recruiting coordinator oversee this procedure. As you participate in on-campus interviews, it is likely you won't know how these decisions are made at each firm.

How Firms Relay Callback Information to Students

If you receive callbacks from firms with which you interview on-campus, you'll receive the news in different ways. In some firms, a partner will call and formally invite you to the firm. In some cases, if you really impressed a firm, you may even receive this invitation during the on-campus interview, but this is not the norm, and placement offices discourage this practice. Many firms simply mail you a letter indicating that they would like to invite you back to the firm for further interviews. Often, this letter is accompanied by a set of instructions for making your travel arrangements, including guidelines about what the firm will and will not pay for. Other firms will simply ask that you contact a particular person in the firm to make these arrangements. Many more students, however, receive "rejection" letters. These are also referred to as "ding" letters and have wallpapered many law students' bathrooms.

Responding to Callbacks

Always respond quickly and courteously to callback invitations. You have no way of knowing how many students are being called back to a firm, how many interview slots exist, and what a firm's timetable is. Responding quickly is especially important if your school suspends classes for a callback week. Some firms limit the number of students it interviews each day to just a few people. If you are from a big school with a callback week, such as Harvard or Stanford, and many of your classmates are called back to a firm, there may be more students than interview slots available. And sometimes firms simply run out of interview space. You should also assume that students from other schools will be interviewing during the same week. Planning ahead will make your visit run smoother.

Your advance planning can have a positive economic impact, which firms also appreciate as recruiting budgets continue to shrink. A student can often save a firm hundreds or even thousands of dollars by planning ahead. While you won't get hired only because you saved the firm money by purchasing a supersaver fare, being courteous, even from an economic standpoint, usually doesn't go unnoticed.

7

THE IN-HOUSE INTERVIEW

"Frankly, we're looking for a crop of associates who will work
their butts off and make us a pile of dough, then move on."

The in-house interview is the "meat" of the recruiting process. This stage
of the recruiting cycle requires a substantial amount of time and energy
and is also the most stressful part. The best advice I can give to you at this
stage of the game is to plan, prepare, and listen to what your intuition tells
you.

Firms handle the in-house interview process in different ways. Most
medium to large firms will fly you to their office, put you up at a nice hotel,
feed you extremely well, and roll out the red carpet to impress you. Smaller
firms will be less formal and extravagant in their approach. As you talk with
multiple firms, the variations between them will either be extremely subtle or
be staring you in the face, so pay attention to what goes on around you during this process, as a big decision must be made at the end—where you want
to work—and you'll be surprised how everything runs together after a while.

MAKING TRAVEL ARRANGEMENTS

If you are looking outside the area of your law school, you'll be faced with
making travel arrangements. Making these arrangements is a relatively simple exercise, but if you fumble in this elementary task, it could have an adverse effect on your chances of getting an offer. Play it safe and follow
directions from the start.

Reimbursable Expenses

The majority of firms reimburse second-year students for travel expenses related to callback interviews. The following expenses are usually reimbursable:

- Airfare (economy class)
- Mileage reimbursement if you drive to the interview
- Transportation from your school to the airport
- Ground transportation once you arrive at your destination
- Hotel expenses
- Meals
- Parking fees, tolls, etc.
- Local phone calls

If a firm doesn't mention travel reimbursement when the interview is arranged, ask them if they reimburse students for callbacks. If they do, ask what specific expenses they'll reimburse for and how to go about making your arrangements. Large firms, typically, don't differ that much in what they will and will not pay for. Small firms, with smaller recruiting budgets, may not have the resources to roll out the red carpet in the manner that large firms do.

What Firms Won't Pay For

Never abuse the privilege of having a firm put you up in an elegant hotel or flying you across the country for interviews. As recruiting budgets shrink, recruiting coordinators are watching for possible abuses in the process like hawks. Typically, firms won't reimburse students for the following expenses and have been known to make students repay them for these abuses:

- Video rentals in hotels
- Long-distance phone calls (although one or two is probably okay)
- Valet parking
- Laundry services
- Meals for other people
- Business or first-class airfares
- In-room minibar expenses
- Bar bills
- Meals at extravagant restaurants

Making Your Own Arrangements

There are steps you need to take when making your own travel arrangements:

1. *Obtain a reimbursement form.* Firms should give you a travel reimbursement form either when they send you a letter formally inviting you to the firm for interviews, when they confirm your interview date in writing (if they do this), or during the actual interview process. If not, ask for one.
2. *If interviewing with multiple firms in the same city, make your arrangements through one firm only.* Give your completed form to the same firm, along with a list of the other firms you interviewed with during that trip. They will take care of getting reimbursed from each other.
3. *Make your trip economical.* Schedule your interviews so that you visit as many firms in one trip as possible. Firms appreciate students making this kind of effort. In addition, recruiting professionals talk among themselves, and it's likely that they'll uncover the student who flies east every Friday to interview with only one firm so he can maintain his bicoastal romance. Firms have little tolerance for this type of behavior.
4. *Don't jump the gun and make arrangements with your own travel agent before you contact the firm you're going to interview with.* Many firms have worked out deals with hotels and airlines and often save money by using certain travel agents, airlines, hotels, and so on. Respect the wishes of the firm that is paying for your trip.

Getting Reimbursed

There are a few simple guidelines you should follow when getting reimbursed for your travel expenses:

1. *Be prompt in your request for reimbursement.* Some firms have put a thirty-day limit on reimbursement—you have to send in your expense form within thirty days of the interview or you will not be reimbursed. It is simply common courtesy not to wait sixty or ninety days for reimbursement. Besides, most students need to be reimbursed promptly so they can pay their own bills.
2. *Keep good records.* Firms are required by law to have receipts for expenditures over a certain dollar amount. **Always** ask for receipts, even for the smallest expense. This also makes your record keeping much easier in the end.
3. *Firms should also be prompt in reimbursing you for your out-of-pocket expenses.* If you don't receive a check within three weeks, call the recruiting coordinator or office administrator. Letters sometimes get lost in the mail, or paperwork gets backed up on someone's desk. That is a lame excuse, but it does happen.

IN-HOUSE INTERVIEW ETIQUETTE (OR WHAT EMILY POST WOULD TELL LAW STUDENTS)

In-house interviewing is a two-way street. You're there to check out the firm, and the firm, in turn, is looking you over as a potential employee. Using the proper etiquette during the process is vital to your success. Too many students don't know what they should and shouldn't do during this process. And the details make a world of difference, from your end as well as the firm's. Here are some crucial pointers for you to follow as you go through the in-house interview process:

1. *Always be on time.* Being late, while sometimes outside of your control, is simply rude. Be at the firm fifteen minutes early. It's not necessary to be there any earlier than that. If you're going to be more than fifteen minutes late, find a way to call the firm and tell them. No-shows are inexcusable.

2. *Call attorneys and professional staff members by their formal names.* Even in an informal setting, refer to all attorneys and staff members by "Mr. Smith" or "Ms. Williams" unless instructed otherwise.

3. *Stand up when others enter an office.* This sounds formal and outdated, but you'll be surprised how many people appreciate this display of respect and courtesy. You don't see this too often anymore.

4. *Shake hands firmly.* Always stick your hand out when introduced to someone, and shake firmly, without using the Arnold Schwarzenegger grip. Nothing turns people off more than a weak, limp handshake or a power grip. Many job offers have been lost on this one.

5. *Treat the staff with respect.* You never know how influential the support staff is in a firm until you work there, so you should never underestimate their clout. Be as nice and courteous to the nonlawyers as to the lawyers.

6. *Never drink alcohol during an interview lunch or dinner.* It's inappropriate to order wine, beer, or mixed drinks at an interview meal, even if everyone else at the table is ordering. I would also restrain during the cocktail hour unless you feel relaxed enough with the group around you.

7. *Be courteous and respectful at all times.* If you quickly decide that this isn't the firm for you, act as if it is while you're there. It's amazing how small the legal community is. Recruiting professionals know one another, and they talk. If you act like a jerk at one firm, that news can easily find its way around town. And you never know when you will end up sitting at the same table as the partner you acted like a jerk toward in an interview.

8. *Be yourself.* You won't fit in a place that clashes with who and what you are. Don't change who you are to adapt to a completely new environment.

9. *Treat the recruiting coordinator with dignity and respect.* Most students don't realize how much clout some recruiting coordinators have in the hiring process. Being rude or disrespectful to them can be your kiss of death.

10. *Always return phone calls to the firm.* Even if you decide you're not interested in a firm, return their phone calls to you, anyway. You never know why a firm is calling, and it's simply rude not to return your phone calls.

11. *Never cancel interviews at the last minute.* Many a smug second-year has called to cancel a 10:00 A.M. interview at 9:15 A.M. the same morning, thinking that they'll never encounter anyone from that firm again. WRONG. The law firm community is very small, even in the largest cities. Word gets around, and the hiring partner at the firm you shafted at the last minute may end up one day as the lead partner in your work group! Attorneys, like elephants, never forget.

HOW THE CALLBACK INTERVIEW PROCESS WORKS

It's helpful to understand how the callback process works at firms before you begin your in-house interviews. You'll be much more comfortable and at ease if you have a general idea of what's going to happen when you visit firms.

Whom You'll See and How Long It Takes

You'll encounter a multitude of approaches to the callback interview process when you visit law firms. During callbacks, expect to meet a variety of attorneys, from the most junior associate to the most senior partner. If you expressed a strong interest in a particular practice area, anticipate seeing at least one or two attorneys from that area. Often, you'll be treated to lunch or dinner or, in rare cases, both. Some firms interview students for half days; others take even more time. Just remember that this will be an exhausting exercise, especially if you have scheduled weeks of back-to-back interviews.

Don't be disappointed or take it personally if, during the interview process, you do not get to speak with the attorneys with whom you particularly wanted to talk. Do not be concerned if you do not talk with a partner or associate in a particular practice area, especially if there are only one or two people in that area. Many students come in for interviews specifically wanting to talk to a specific partner, only to discover that partner is busy with clients or out of the country. Interviewing is important to any firm, but client work will always come first. This is one reason interview schedules frequently change during the course of a day.

Don't be astounded, however, if you're not treated to a meal during the interview process, and don't chalk it up to the myth that "if a firm doesn't take me to lunch, then they must not be interested in me." Firms often have difficulty coaxing busy attorneys to take two hours of their billable day to take recruits to lunch or dinner. The associates want to go home to their families in the evening if they don't have to work late. This is the main reason many firms don't treat recruits to dinner and sometimes skip taking them to lunch.

What Happens Once You Arrive

When you arrive, ask for the recruiting coordinator or whomever your contact is. In some firms, your interviews will begin immediately. At others, you will talk first with the recruiting coordinator, hiring partner, or a member of the firm's hiring committee. Often, you are given a list of the attorneys you're scheduled to meet, along with their biographical profiles. Other firms give you this information at the end of the day in case of schedule changes. If you don't receive this information, ask for a list of the attorneys you interviewed with before you leave the firm.

THINGS TO LOOK FOR DURING THE INTERVIEW

Before you begin the in-house interview process, you should have a general idea of what things you should be looking for. Don't go into the situation blind, afterward wishing you had known what to look out for.

What's the Office Environment Like?

While visiting firms, get a good feel for the office environment, both for aesthetics and intangibles. The external environment of a firm tells you a lot. Ask yourself the following questions as you walk around the halls and meet various people:

- What impression does the firm give you while sitting in the lobby?
- What conversations are taking place around you?

- Do all employees appear happy and content?
- Do people speak to one another while passing in the halls?
- Does the firm seem like a pleasant place to work?
- Does the firm appear to be efficiently run, or is it still in the dark ages?

It's often more revealing to meet with attorneys in their own offices than in a central conference room. Notice what type of offices associates are given. Does everyone have a modern computer and telephone? Are support staff members treated like second-class citizens, while partners have lavish offices the size of many apartments? Is the office dingy, in dire need of renovation? (This could signal that the firm is having economic problems.) What type of library resources are available? How big is the support staff? Pick up on what is going on around you, and let your intuition be your guide.

When speaking with partners and senior associates, ask yourself, is this someone I would enjoy working with, would like taking orders from, and would respect? You really have to respect the people in a firm, and firms attract different types of people. For example, one firm interviewed the son of a well-known entertainer. His grades were mediocre, but he had attended excellent schools all of his life and had many experiences unusual for someone his age. During the interview, he kept dropping the names of famous people he knew on a first-name basis. For some firms, these connections would be very useful. But this particular firm was full of self-made attorneys who had thrived in their careers without help from a well-known father. Therefore, his name-dropping turned off most people at the firm. While this firm didn't call him back, many firms found the well-connected son of a famous professional a strong addition. Different firms look for different types of people.

Look out for red flags as you go through the interview process. If everything sounds too good to be true, then it probably is. Most law firms require complete dedication, long hours, hard work, and your firstborn child. Beware if a firm makes promises that aren't the norm. If they tell you that they have no billable hour requirements, that only means that they aren't written down in the firm handbook. Also, don't believe anyone who tells you that everyone (except the support staff) usually works nine to five. Don't be gullible as you go through this process. Large firms do not pay huge salaries so you can work forty or fifty hours a week. Educate yourself before going in so that you know when something deviates from the norm.

Work Distribution and Training

Find out how work is handed out and what level of attorneys summer associates typically work with. As an associate, would you rarely work side by side with a partner, or would you work routinely with a partner early on? If training is important to you, find out how much training is provided for summer associates and young associates. Some firms routinely provide elaborate training sessions. Others adopt an indoctrination by fire attitude. Do you need hand-holding, or do you want to hit the ground running from day one? You should have an idea of which method suits your personality the best.

ASK GOOD QUESTIONS

Always bring a set of prepared questions to the interview, even if you don't use them. Bring a notebook with you, preferably a legal pad with a leather cover. Make sure it's professional-looking. Your questions should be written down—typed or handwritten—it doesn't matter. You have them with you if you need them, and there is nothing wrong with referring to your questions during an interview. You will appear prepared and interested in the firm—you've done your homework. Have two sets of questions in mind—some that are suitable for associates and another set just for partners. Attorneys often think that you aren't interested in their firm if you don't ask questions about it. Demonstrate that you are interested and that you've done a little background research. It will impress them.

Don't Let Partners Intimidate Your Ability to Ask Questions

Be assertive when you ask partners questions, especially the very tough questions. Partners are just people and are just as approachable as any associate. Avoid "canned" questions that come across as rehearsed and recycled. And never kiss up to partners during an interview. They know when you are doing this despite what you might think, and most do not like it. Just pretend that partners have the same clout as the associates throughout the interview process. For all you know, they do.

Be Creative but Not Fanatical

Use your creativity, indicating that you have done your homework without going overboard. You may appear desperate if you know too much about a firm. Being fanatical won't help your chances of getting an offer. Ask a few thought-provoking questions that indicate you are seriously interested in the firm. For example, it's not necessary to know the complete history of a firm or to know what was in the legal press yesterday. It won't impress anyone if you are knowledgeable about the firm's history. They'll only query why you have so much available time to research information that is really useless for the interview process.

The flip side is that you should be aware of any recent important developments in a firm. If an important government official recently joined the firm or if the firm recently merged with another well-known firm, you should know that.

Some Sample Questions

The following is a list of possible interview questions that can be molded to fit most firms, *once you have completed your research on the firm.* Tailor your questions to each firm you interview with.

- What made the difference when you decided to join this firm, or how is this firm different from others you considered?
- Expound on your most challenging assignment thus far in your career here.
- What are some of the common attributes members of this firm possess?
- Is the training satisfactory? What changes would you make? Describe a recent training program. Is all training done in-house? In what areas does the training need to be improved?
- What are the best and worst aspects of working here? (Make sure that the interview is going well enough to use this one. Be very positive when you pose this question.)
- Describe a typical day. What do you like the least and the most about your current routine at the firm?
- What is the firm's vision for the future? Does the firm possess a mission statement? If so, how often is that goal or vision altered? (Ask only partners this one.)
- Does the firm teach associates networking and marketing skills? If so, how is this achieved?
- When does the firm expect associates to start building their own client base?
- What are the biggest mistakes associates make in their careers in this firm? (This is another question only for partners or very senior associates.)
- How do you envision technology being utilized in the firm in the future? (This is a good questions for any "techy" attorney you meet.)
- What was the biggest surprise once you joined the firm? How is your position different from what you expected?
- What are the firm's strengths and weaknesses? How are the weaknesses being addressed?

Topics You Shouldn't Broach

It is essential that you ask intelligent and insightful questions during the interview process. Just as important, however, is avoiding certain questions or topics that may be inappropriate, are in bad taste, or should be common sense. The following topics and questions should be completely avoided during the interview process:

- Don't ask for information on maternity and paternity leave. While it is illegal to discriminate against individuals in their childbearing years, firms do sometimes think along these lines. If you have to obtain information on this subject, refer to the firm's National Association for Law Placement form, or contact the personnel director incognito. Asking about paternity leave, even though many firms have paternity leave policies in place, can be the kiss of death in the male-dominated law firm culture.
- Don't inquire about how many students are being interviewed or which students from your school are being interviewed. This really does not concern you.
- Don't expound on your desire to perform pro bono work, asking what the firm's policy is regarding the amount of pro bono work an associate can perform. If you have an interest in pro bono work, keep it to yourself during the interview process. Firms have different philosophies regarding pro bono work, and until you know for sure what the firm's philosophy is, you are better off keeping your charitable interests to yourself.
- Do not ask questions that may make the firm appear as though it is behind the technology curve, even if it is.
- Never ask what hours you are expected to work. This indicates that you are concerned that you might have to work long hours. I guarantee that you will.
- Never ask what the billable hour requirement is. If there is a written requirement, it is on the NALP form. In a large or medium-sized firm, you can assume that the minimum is at least 1,500 hours and, more than likely, much higher than that.
- Avoid questions about attrition rates. You do not want to put the interviewer or firm on the defensive. Ask the recruiting coordinator directly about this.
- Questions that are in the rumor mill about the firm should be avoided. You do not want to come across as someone who is involved in law school or law firm gossip. And very often, rumors are just that—rumors.
- Save your questions about salary and benefits until the appropriate time. While you want to make an informed decision, asking about salary and benefits too early can make it appear as though you think you're getting

an offer. Refer to a firm's NALP form for this information, or ask the recruiting coordinator or office administrator, off the record.

MISTAKES TO AVOID

I'm astounded by the mistakes students make during the in-house interview process. Regardless of what school they go to or how intelligent they are, they say the wrong things, make stupid moves, and often don't use common sense. These problems can be completely avoided, however. I'm going to spell it out for you here, giving you examples of some of the blunders I'm talking about. Many of my instructions may seem like common sense. Well, I thought so too until I saw these blatant errors demonstrated time and again.

Tactics You Should Shy Away From

1. *Indicating you're interested in areas of law that you have no interest in.* Students, in an effort to be agreeable and get a job, say they're interested in areas of practice that don't interest them at all. Don't tell people only what they want to hear! If you make this mistake you may be in for a long summer. Be honest with yourself and with the firm with which you're interviewing. If not, you may be stuck doing something you hate.
2. *Spreading yourself too thin.* This applies particularly to the stellar candidates who have little trouble securing interviews. You may not realize that in "stacking the deck" by taking as many interviews with as many firms as possible, you are wasting much of your own valuable time and that of the busy attorneys who take time to interview you. You don't need to interview with every large firm in San Francisco just to ensure that you have ten job offers to choose from. Only interview with firms you have a strong interest in from the very beginning. But even more important is the fact that you, by interviewing with every firm on both coasts, may be taking interview slots from your less fortunate peers who don't have as many choices as you do.
3. *Acting like a stud.* In other words, don't be a stud. One student from a very prestigious law school with an unbelievable record was invited to attend a firm's weekly Friday evening cocktail party. The firm regularly included the staff at this function. The student, while mingling with the partners and associates, asked a paralegal out for a date. She quickly turned him down, so he then asked out another staff member. Needless to say, the firm was not amused by the student's lack of decorum and his dating techniques.

4. *Wearing your future plans on your chest.* Keep your future plans to yourself. A student from a very good law school, while interviewing in-house with a firm, told several attorneys during the process that he had no interest in working for any firm longer than two years, since it was his intention to eventually work as an attorney in a major corporation. While there are probably thousands of students in law schools with similar plans, don't go into a law firm wearing that message on your chest. He insulted many people and wasted a lot of the firm's money. While there may be some big firms who don't care if students leave after two or three years, because many of them do, the majority of firms don't appreciate this kind of attitude. Keep your long-term plans to yourself if they don't include staying with a firm at least until you see what your partnership prospects look like, even though this plan may not be realistic in today's job market.

5. *Assuming people don't have influence when they do.* Never underestimate the clout that anyone in a firm may have in the recruiting process. This includes secretaries, members of the recruiting staff, and associates. One Yale student wrongly assumed that the two associates he lunched with didn't have the influence to keep him, with his amazing credentials, from getting a summer job offer. Amazingly, during lunch, this student emptied two jars of raw sugar packets into his pockets while dining at a three-star restaurant. Apparently, raw sugar packets are a hot commodity in New Haven. The associates were astounded by his social skills and were on the phone to the hiring partner and recruiting coordinator the minute they returned to the office. Needless to say, the Yale student did not receive a job offer. Recollection of the incident, however, provided hours of entertainment at firm recruiting meetings for weeks.

6. *Not treating all firms you encounter with dignity and respect.* Some students, once they decide where they want to work, quit returning phone calls or, in the worst case scenario, fail to respond to job offers and leave firms hanging, often for months. This type of behavior can only hurt you as well as your peers, who might have received the job offer you never responded to. Yes, this does happen. Don't burn your bridges, as the law firm community is just too small and you never know where you might end up. Too many students, either out of ignorance or inexperience, make this mistake over and over again, and it can come back to haunt you. The nice guys don't always finish first.

LAW FIRMS MAKE BLUNDERS, TOO

Practicing attorneys make interviewing mistakes perhaps more often than law students. It's probable that during the in-house interview process you'll be subjected to an occasional whim of an interviewing attorney who may think he's playing by the rules. Others don't care if they abide by the rules or not. And I can think of numerous examples where someone remained within the bounds of the law but exercised really poor judgment during an interview. I'll give you some examples. They have great entertainment value.

The experience of one Georgetown University student paints a very negative picture of one law firm. This second-year female student interviewed with a successful female partner in a prestigious law firm. The partner began the twenty-minute interview only to get up during the session, walk down the hall to the rest room, bringing the student with her. She kept the interview going, without interruption, while she used the bathroom and walked back down the hall to her office, as if nothing out of the ordinary had taken place. While the partner's time management skills are excellent, her interviewing technique needs a little work. The student was horrified by the partner's tactless manners and had zero interest in spending a summer at that firm.

Another story involves two associates who interviewed a second-year student at a medium-sized firm in northern Virginia. The two associates interviewed the candidate at the same time. One of the associates attended the same undergraduate school as the student and managed to carry on a very hospitable and interesting conversation. But the other associate kept picking words off the candidate's resume and continually asked him, during the interview, if he was sure these words were spelled correctly. The student was positive that there were no misspelled words on his resume and was quite annoyed. But to make the situation go from bad to worse, the associate pulled out the dictionary during the interview and started to check the words one by one. As the student had stated, there were no misspelled words. The student walked away from the interview extremely annoyed and with zero interest in that law firm.

FOLLOWING UP AFTER THE
INTERVIEW

I can't impress on you enough how important it is to follow up with a firm following your visit there. It's probably more important to follow up now than it is after an on-campus interview, which we talked about in Chapter 3. Good etiquette says you should send a thank-you note even if you're not interested in the firm. Follow the same procedures for sending thank-you notes as we discussed in depth in Chapter 3. You just never know where you might run into an attorney you met along the interview trail later on. And good manners never go out of style.

Timing is key, so make sure you mail your letter within a week of your interview, even if you're on the road. Just carry a box of good letter writing paper with you. You'll always be safe using buff or white Crane notes, and you can buy a box inexpensively at any stationery store. If you spoke with five or more attorneys, send a note to one person, asking him or her to forward a copy to others in the firm. Or you can send a letter to the recruiting coordinator or her counterpart, asking him or her to do the same.

SUMMER HIRING DECISIONS

Evaluating students at the in-house interview is an uncomplicated process. Each firm estimates how many offers it needs to make to hire their optimal number of summer associates. Believe me, in many instances, it's just a "crapshoot." Firms never know what their acceptance rate is going to be, and you hear horror stories (for the recruiting coordinator, anyway) such as the large New York firm that had a surprisingly high acceptance rate and ended up with a summer program of 60 law students, much to the dismay of the 60 students—many of whom weren't hired. But usually firms know enough about their past history to gauge how many offers they need to extend to fill their summer class. Smaller firms tend to make one or two offers and then wait until the offers are accepted or rejected before extending additional offers.

How Students Are Evaluated

As you come through a firm, written evaluations are completed by the interviewing attorneys. It's almost like going to a wine tasting and filling out a form on each wine you taste, keeping in mind how much you liked the wines you've already tasted. Often firms create their own evaluation forms. At Baker & McKenzie, we used the same evaluation form for all law school candidates.

Completed evaluations are sent to the recruiting coordinator or counterpart, who tabulates them for the hiring committee or whomever is making the hiring decisions. Rarely does anyone receive 100 percent "recommend for immediate hiring." But rarely will you rate "do not recommend" from everyone you interview with. Usually, you end up somewhere in the middle. It takes a lot to impress attorneys. They also prefer to keep intangible, intuitive, or "gut" feelings about prospective candidates to themselves, so they're often called on to elaborate on their spartan comments.

CANDIDATE EVALUATION FORM

Interviewee _____ Date of Interview _____

School/Firm/Agency _____

Position _____

Section I
Please complete this section based on the following 5-point scale:

1. Verbal ability	_____	5 — Outstanding
2. Confidence and poise	_____	4 — Above average
3. Personality	_____	3 — Average
4. Motivation	_____	2 — Below average
5. Demeanor	_____	1 — Unacceptable
6. Long-term commitment to Washington area	_____	X — Unable to evaluate from interview
7. Valuable experience	_____	
8. Intellectual ability	_____	

Section II
Please check below:

I recommend for immediate hiring. _____

I have no reservations regarding hiring. _____

I have reservations regarding hiring. (*Please comment below.*) _____

This candidate should not be considered further for hiring. (Please comment below.) _____

Section III
Please comment:

_____

_____

_____

Signed _____

The Hiring Committee's Part in the Process

Law firm hiring committees meet weekly or biweekly—whatever it takes—during the busy recruiting season to make decisions about candidates. While the process varies in every firm, hiring committees often are blessed with the task of selecting summer associate candidates, monitoring the acceptance rate, and following up with students who have outstanding offers. This can be a full-time job if a firm anticipates having a large summer program.

During hiring committee meetings, the attorneys discuss candidates based on the completed evaluation forms from the interview process. If necessary, references are sometimes checked on "borderline" candidates or for clarification on a candidate's past work history or academic record. Often students are put on "hold," waiting for other candidates to come through, waiting for students to decline or accept offers, or simply because a committee can't make a decision on a candidate. Being put on hold is not a sign of weakness, nor does it demonstrate a lack of interest in your candidacy. It's often a result of timing, so don't despair when you don't hear from a firm. At this point, assume that no news is good news. Nevertheless, every firm handles this process a little bit differently, with the same of goal of hiring the best and the brightest students.

Courting Students

Some firms heavily court students during the summer associate hiring process, while others don't. Much depends on the personality of a firm, its hiring goals, and in some cases, how badly a firm wants to hire a candidate. We've all heard of firms that call students every three days attempting to get them to accept the offer or firms that are constantly taking students out to lunch, dinner, or for cocktails as a recruiting tool. Other firms simply have the attitude that if a student really likes us and really wants to work for us, then the frills aren't necessary.

One large litigation firm actively courts its recruits, calling them two or three times a week. This behavior is a reflection of the character of the firm—an aggressive working atmosphere, where everyone is expected to go for the gusto. The firm looks favorably on candidates who like this type of persistent personality. Another well-known firm has the completely opposite attitude. This firm prefers the self-motivated personality who doesn't need or want to be stroked. They rarely make multiple phone calls to recruits and prefer not to wine and dine candidates. But they often get the students they want using this approach because it works for them.

8

SECOND-YEAR HIRING IN SMALL FIRMS

"I would have been on law review, but I wasn't."

I've talked a lot about how large and medium-sized firms hire students for their summer programs. But your chances of landing a law firm position are much greater in a small firm than in a large firm, simply because more hiring is being done in small firms than in large ones. Usually the stakes aren't as high, and the credential factor isn't as big an issue with the small firms, so your chances of getting hired are greater as well.

Except for a brief period from 1988 to 1990, small firms have consistently been the single most important source for graduates entering private practice. Since 1990, apart from solo practice, only firms of two to ten attorneys have consistently increased their representation in the pool of initial jobs obtained in private practice, according to the National Association for Law Placement. Small firms are the most important source of employment for new law school graduates, especially for those students without stellar academic records from top law schools.

The NALP estimates that almost half of all law firm jobs are now being taken with firms of 25 or fewer attorneys. This is compared to the 3.5 percent of jobs obtained with the largest firms, 501+ attorneys. According to the placement director at one well-known Washington, D.C., law school, half of her students from the class of 1995 went to work in law firms. Of that 50 percent, 60 percent went to work in small law firms. And that number continues to grow. The "smolo," small or solo firm, is becoming a mainstay in the legal placement landscape.

WHAT SMALL FIRMS LOOK FOR

Unlike their large firm counterparts, small firms lack the resources and the need to plan months or even years in advance for anticipated growth in attorney personnel. Placement directors typically report that small firms hire "all over the map," which makes it difficult to establish a plan for recruiting. Students complain that there is little information available on small firms, which makes their recruiting efforts much more difficult. Many do not have summer programs, and they often wait to hire new graduates until after they take the bar exam. This creates a big dilemma for students—much of the law firm hiring is taking place in small firms, but there is little information available on how to go about getting these positions.

The characteristics and credential set needed to be successful in a small firm are quite different from those needed in large law firm environments. Your internal assessment should indicate which type of environment, large or small, suits your personality type best. Are you happier being a small fish in a big pond (a specialist), or are you happier being a big fish in a little pond, such as in a small law firm environment?

Small firms typically look for flexible, well-rounded individuals who are able to wear many hats and who immediately "fit" into their particular culture. A "do whatever needs to be done" attitude is essential in a smaller environment, where attorneys sometimes have to act as lawyer, administrator, paralegal, courier, receptionist, and so on. There is little need for the "specialist" mentality in a small law firm. You may be a litigator one day and have to write a will and perform a real estate closing the next day. There is also little tolerance for the "spoiler" mentality in a small firm. The difficult personality, who can be tossed to a back office in a larger firm to do research, never to be seen again, has nowhere to hide in a small firm. Getting along with everyone is essential in a small firm environment.

One partner, who had worked in a large firm and now has his own five-attorney firm, stresses the importance of camaraderie in a small firm, noting, "I have two families—my wife and children, and my law firm." Larger firms tend to hire people they like, but that's not as essential as in a small firm. This partner also stresses the importance the staff plays in a small firm. If an associate or summer associate can't get along with the staff, he or she will not last long in a small firm. In more rural areas, where you many find only one or two practitioners in a firm, these factors are magnified.

Small firms also tend to hire for the long term, which isn't as realistic in larger firms. Because smaller firms hire fewer attorneys, they are more careful and have less resources to devote to hiring mistakes. They can't afford the turnover rates that are becoming the norm in the big firms. Long-term fit, therefore, is extremely important.

DO THE RESEARCH

Since the lack of information available on small firms is a universal problem that isn't likely to disappear, you must learn to take the initiative to crack the small firm market. You can't lean too much on your placement office in this effort. Learning to take the initiative is time-consuming, and only with persistence will your endeavors yield satisfactory results. But you have a lot of options. The small firm market, while difficult to get a firm grasp of, is penetrable.

Narrow Your Focus

Your first step in researching small firms is to narrow your focus geographically. You'll probably be more successful if you select an area where you have a previous connection. It's more likely that you'll want to work somewhere that's familiar or where you know someone. Students often return to their hometowns or go to areas where they have friends or relatives. But make sure you select several areas to concentrate on from the very beginning.

Research Your Market in Person

Once you have targeted your location, take the time to go there and spend time researching the law firm market. Since printed information on the small firms is scarce, your next best resource is meeting the attorneys in person and talking to members of the community who are familiar with the local market. The information you need is available, but the best way to retrieve it is through primary research.

Your networking skills are your most useful resource as you search for leads in a small community. Go to the local bar association, the chamber of commerce, and local professional organizations such as the Rotary Club or the Lions Club. Go to the courthouse and talk to the clerk of court, the register of deeds, and so on to find out who the main players are in the legal community. Getting these individuals' attention over the phone may be difficult, since they wear many hats, so stop by their offices in person. This tactic tends to be better accepted in smaller communities, where people tend, overall, to be more friendly. I may have given the impression that it's inappropriate to take the "sales rep approach" when contacting *all* firms, since the large firms shun the practice. I encourage you to call on the small firms in person because it's the best way to meet those who have the authority to hire you in this market.

One student from St. Louis who was in the middle of his class at an average East Coast law school looked up all of the attorneys in St. Louis who had attended his undergraduate school and high school. He used an alumnae directory as well as *Martindale-Hubbell,* a well-known directory of attorneys that is organized by state, to do his research. His next step was to go to St. Louis and do the rest of his research in person. Using this approach, he obtained a job working 25 hours a week for an attorney who, in fact, attended both of his alma maters.

Other Helpful Hints

Organizing your approach toward small firms is difficult at best, but this is a virtually untapped resource in the legal job market. Use it to your advantage. The following are some additional tips that may assist you in your search:

1. *Network and network some more.* Networking and the luck of being at the right place at the right time are the two greatest predictors of success for getting into a small firm. The adage "It's who you know" applies here in full force. If a firm is only hiring one or two people, usually those people are recommended by someone the firm knows and trusts. And simply being lucky has its place in law firm hiring.

2. *Offer to work for free.* If you're from a community where small firms exist in abundance, use personal contacts to get your foot in the door. Over the winter holiday break, contact these firms, and stop by for a visit or informational interview. Offer to work a week or so over the holiday for free to show them what you can do. If you can't afford to work for free for the summer, perhaps you could work for the firm part of the time. At the very least, you may come into contact with other attorneys in the community who may be interested in hiring a new associate in the near future.

3. *Work for Legal Aid or any nonprofit organization in the community.* To increase your visibility, do volunteer work for a local nonprofit organization to get noticed by area lawyers. You may have to do this during your first-year summer, over a holiday break, or during the school year if proximity allows. This is also a great way to network and make the connections necessary to land an associate position if you are not already connected. There are always organizations that need free manpower, es-

pecially from an aspiring attorney. Besides, you can gain valuable work experience in the process.

4. *Utilize resume drops.* A less effective way to get a position in a smaller firm is through a resume drop at your placement office. Small to medium-sized firms often request resumes from schools as an alternative to visiting the campus. Small firms typically recruit from schools in their general area. With this method, however, you're playing a numbers game. And resumes are being reviewed, often, by someone who hires only occasionally, so less obvious traits on a resume may get passed over. Many small firms hire using this method, but the odds are probably not on your side.

5. *Clerk during the school year.* Working as a law clerk during the school year is a common practice during the second and third years of law school in many areas. This is an excellent way to gain solid law firm experience and to make contacts in the legal community, especially in small firms. If you have a successful working relationship with a firm after six or eight months and express a strong interest in working for them, your chances of getting a summer job offer may be much greater. Clerking is also an excellent way to gain experience. But clerking can backfire if your experience in the firm is less than good or you do a mediocre job. I'll talk about this option in more detail in Chapter 9.

9

OTHER ENTRÉES INTO SUMMER PROGRAMS

"I'm not a law student, as you can see. I'm looking for an illegal position."

There are additional avenues into summer programs that we haven't discussed yet. One possibility is to work as a paralegal first for a few years before attending law school. Another option is work as a law clerk in a firm during the school year before joining a summer program. These alternatives offer no guarantees of job offers and may even add a few years to your journey through law school, but I'll show you examples of students who landed great jobs through these avenues. This exposure also enabled them to make an enlightened decision about where they truly wanted to work—an exposure that their summer associate peers didn't have.

THE PARALEGAL ROUTE

Lots of people work as paralegals before attending law school. But most never use their experience to lay the groundwork for something bigger and better later on. There are some paralegals who become so valuable to their law firms, through their dedication and quality of work, that they depart for law school with an open invitation to come back to the firm as a summer associate or even associate.

This option may sound simple or obvious, but to make yourself valuable enough to a law firm to walk away with an open ticket to return at a higher level, you have to pay a price. The majority of paralegals, regardless of their educational background and intelligence, aren't willing to ante up what it takes to receive such an open invitation. And some would prefer to work in another firm or another location. But let me give you a real-life example of what I'm talking about.

The Story of the Telecommunications Paralegal

A firm in a large East Coast city hired a recent college graduate to work as a telecommunications paralegal. He had slightly better than average grades from a prestigious state university. He wasn't a member of Phi Beta Kappa or even on the dean's list. He was the first paralegal dedicated to telecommunications that the firm had ever hired, so there were a lot of unknown factors about him and the position itself. They weren't exactly sure what they really needed for this position but knew that they needed someone at this level working in the telecommunications area.

The telecommunications paralegal, over a period of two to three years, managed to become one of the most valuable members of the firm's telecommunications practice. The quality of his work was exceptional. The hours he put in astounded even the most dedicated associates and partners. He did the work of two people, and when he finally decided to enter law school, the firm was at a loss as to how to replace him. He decided to attend a local law school in his home state, one that the law firm never recruited from. But when the former paralegal needed a summer job during his second summer, he had only to pick up the phone and call a few partners at his former law firm. They immediately offered him a job, and he ultimately joined the firm as an associate.

The Amount of Dedication It Really Takes

But how much dedication does it take to get in the door this way, and how long do you need to work as a paralegal in a firm to carve out this type of relationship? There are no magic answers here, but I'll give you another example.

Another firm told me the story of a paralegal who possessed the same level of dedication as the telecommunications paralegal we just talked about. She also worked in a sophisticated area of the law, doing much of her work on Excel spreadsheets. She also attended a prestigious state university and planned to attend either law or business school in the near future.

Her work ethic was extraordinary. Not only was the quality of her work exceptional, but also the quantity was amazing. For example, in one month, she billed 360 hours, most of it working on Excel spreadsheets. To quantify those hours, if she billed 360 hours, she probably worked about 375 to 400 hours. That means that she worked 12 hours a day for the entire month, without a day off, on Excel spreadsheets! That, alone, is an amazing feat. She established a strong reputation for herself at her law firm and probably has what it takes be a successful attorney in the firm as well. But she has paid a price—basically her life has been her work for the past few years.

My point is that it takes an extremely high level of dedication and a high quality of work to impress a firm to the point of giving you an open ticket to return, regardless of where you decide to attend law school. Very few people are willing to make these types of sacrifices on a paralegal's salary (which is usually quite low). But this is another route into a law firm that some choose to take.

WINTER AND SPRING CLERKSHIP PROGRAMS

Many firms sponsor clerkship programs during the winter and spring semesters that enable second- and third-year law students to work part-time during the school semester. The hourly salaries are usually quite good, and students are able to gain excellent work experience as well. Some firms use clerkships as an alternative to hiring temporary attorneys, while others view them as an actual recruiting tool, since they're able to work with you extensively before making hiring decisions.

Minority Clerkship Programs

Minority clerkship programs are also quite popular. Firms commit to hire minority students for at least a semester, enabling students from diverse backgrounds to work in major law firms with very high academic standards. Firms participate in minority programs to increase their minority representation, even if only on a temporary basis. Sometimes these students are picked up by the firms. At the very least, their resumes are enhanced, and they gain valuable work experience.

How the Clerkship Hiring Process Works

Firms typically contact law schools in their area and advertise law clerk positions through the career services office. The placement office posts the position at the school, with a deadline for resume collection. They then send a package of resumes to the firm for review. Firms prescreen the resumes, and candidates are selected to interview. The hiring criteria vary among firms. Grades are still important, but often clerks are hired to work in a particular practice area, so outside experience and particular course work become important as well. Firms are generally more lenient than they are when hiring summer associates. Law clerks are paid on an hourly basis and usually work between ten and twenty hours a week. Salaries vary among firms and geographic locations, but rates tend to be very good.

Using Clerkships as an Entrée into a Firm

Sometimes law clerks are hired for summer associate or associate positions after spending time in a firm. You can make yourself so valuable to a firm that other doors are opened on your behalf that might otherwise have been left closed. But if this is your plan, **never** wear it on your sleeve. Keep your ultimate plans to yourself. As far as you're concerned, your goal is to do good work, make some needed cash, and gain work experience. But keep in mind that some firms have a strict policy on not hiring clerks, eliminating the hope that a winter or spring clerkship will be the ticket to a permanent position, since the hiring criteria are often different.

10

SUMMER ASSOCIATE
JOB OFFERS

"... from clown college, it was a logical step to entertainment law."

The climax of the recruiting season is when you finally hear from the firms you've been interviewing with since early fall. You eagerly, but nervously check your mailbox each day, hoping that you'll find offers instead of rejections. This can be nerve-racking. But there is much to consider during this time, and you need to cover your bases. Should you split your summer between two firms? How much time should you take to make your decision without jeopardizing your offers? What facts should your offer letters contain? I'll lead you through this maze and help you answer these questions so that you cover your bases.

HANDLING MULTIPLE JOB OFFERS

Receiving job offers is an exciting culmination to your months of planning and hard work. But properly handling the job offer process can become sticky if you are faced with multiple deadlines from various employers while also waiting to hear from other firms. Many students are not fortunate enough to find themselves in this enviable position, but there is an art to juggling offers while keeping multiple law firms happy. You should know the etiquette of this process so that you properly keep all of your options open:

1. *Abide by NALP's rules.* Whenever possible, abide by the standards and practices established by the National Association for Law Placement. We discussed these rules in depth in Chapter 2, and a copy of them is located in the Appendix. Even if an employer doesn't follow these guidelines, you should.

2. *Never hold more than four offers at one time.* Receiving multiple offers is a luxury and a privilege that many would love to experience, but if you're one of the more fortunate ones, think about your classmates who may not be sitting pretty. The number of law firm summer positions is finite, and for every offer you receive, there is one less offer available for one of your peers to receive. If you know you're not interested in a firm, turn down the offer as soon as possible. Everyone benefits.

3. *Ask for more time if you need it.* If you're unsure about accepting an offer and are deciding between two firms, it's not unreasonable to ask for additional time to make your decision. Firms are usually reasonable about these requests. If you need an extra week or so to make up your mind, ask for it. All a firm can do is say no.

   Small firms, however, may be more time-sensitive and less flexible when it comes to asking for more time to make decisions. If a firm is hiring only one or two people, then their options may be limited if you turn them down. Keep this in mind when considering the timing and acceptance of offers in small firms, since you may get only one shot in a small firm.

4. *Always respond to a firm when you receive an offer.* Always follow up with firms that make you an offer. You'd be surprised at the number of students who never respond to offers firms give them. Again, you never know where you may encounter someone later in life.

5. *Don't be too concerned about salary and benefit information at the summer associate stage.* A firm's basic salary information is provided on its NALP form. If a current NALP form isn't available, ask the firm for *basic* salary information. Summer associate salaries usually aren't negotiable. When associate offers are handed out, you can negotiate salary and benefit issues.

6. *Find out if the firm pays for summer associate moving or travel expenses.* Ask *now* if you'll be reimbursed for moving your belongings for the summer or if the firm will pay for your air or ground transportation at the beginning and end of the summer. For some large firms, paying for these expenses is standard, but never assume that anything will be paid for. If these expenses are being picked up by the firm, make sure it's put in writing. We'll discuss that shortly.

YOUR OFFER LETTER

As mentioned in Chapter 3, job offers should *always* be put in writing. In any professional position, the pertinent facts about a job should be put down on paper for the benefit of both parties. Summer associate positions are no exception. Your letter should include the following information:

1. *Your salary.* Summer associate salaries are usually quoted weekly. Make sure you are told specifically what your salary will be instead of being quoted something like "$7,000 for the summer." Also included is how often you'll get paid. If you're quoted a weekly figure but the firm pays monthly, make sure you don't lose out in the conversion process. All of these things should be specifically laid out in your letter.

2. *Dates of employment.* Some firms start and end their summer programs on specific days. If this is the case, then the letter should indicate that policy. There may be a policy that you have to start work on a Monday and end on a Friday. Make sure that any specific date requirement is mentioned.

3. *Job function or title.* A brief description of your position should be included, such as "summer associate with primary responsibility to perform general legal research." You want to avoid being hired for one position but ending up doing something else, as discussed in Chapter 3.

4. *Other perks you may receive.* As mentioned earlier in this chapter, any perks such as travel and moving expenses should be specifically outlined. If there is a monetary cap on your moving or travel expenses, your letter should spell it out.

5. *Any other general information that you may need to know ahead of time.* If you are encouraged to bring your laptop with you or if you need to bring sporting equipment, your tuxedo, your passport, and so on, these things may or may not be outlined in your offer letter. If these kinds of things aren't outlined in your offer letter, they should be outlined somewhere else prior to your coming on board.

SPLITTING YOUR SUMMER—THE PROS AND CONS

One dilemma you may be faced with is deciding whether you should spend your summer at one firm or whether you should split your summer in half, working for two firms over the course of the summer. Five to ten years ago, when law firm jobs were in abundance, splitting summers was quite common. But when the tide changed and it became a buyer's market, many firms started to discourage this practice. Today, however, in some parts of the country, splitting summers remains a valid option for many students.

The Pros

1. *You can try out more than one location.* If you're torn between working in Atlanta and Los Angeles, splitting enables you to see two cities during one summer.
2. *You can test out both small firms and big ones in one summer.* If you're not quite sure whether you want to do tax work in a boutique or in a large firm, this option may work well for you. Or if you haven't figured out whether you want to be a big fish in a little pond or a little fish in a big pond, splitting may solve your dilemma.
3. *All of your eggs aren't in one basket.* The biggest advantage to splitting your summer is that it gives you more than one option. If you don't like a firm or you don't receive an offer from one firm, chances are you'll like the other one or receive an offer from one of the two firms. In the current age of economic uncertainty, having more than one option makes sense for a lot of people.

The Cons

1. *In many major metropolitan areas, splitting may not be an option.* New York and Washington, D.C., firms, for example, often sneer at splitting, and many simply won't let you. In smaller markets, where students may be deciding between two very different cities, splitting is more common.
2. *It takes an entire summer to really get to know a firm.* Six weeks often isn't enough time to settle in, get to know the attorneys, and complete multiple projects with a variety of people so that the firm can evaluate you and your work. In smaller, more congenial firms, getting to know a student and his or her abilities takes much less time. At Baker & McKenzie, students are sometimes allowed to split, although the practice is not encouraged. For those students who take this option, by the time they finally feel comfortable and get to know the attorneys, it's time to leave. The students who split in bigger markets often agree that it takes much longer than they anticipated to settle in and feel at home.
3. *Firms sometimes consider students who are splitting less dedicated than those who spend an entire summer with them.* They also know their chance of landing you as an associate is 50 percent less than with students who stay with them for the entire summer.
4. *If you elect to come to a firm for the second half of the summer, they automatically assume that they are your second choice.* It is generally

accepted that you spend the first part of your summer with the firm you're most interested in. The summer tends to wind down in late July and early August, when people tend to take vacations, so May, June, and early July are considered the prime time to be in a firm. If you elect to go to a firm during the second half of the summer, you're perceived, from the very beginning, to be less interested in that firm than in the one you worked with earlier in the summer.

5. *You always run out of time.* Trust me. Students never consider how quickly the time passes, even if you elect to spend the entire summer with one firm. There are always people you wanted to work with, areas of practice you wanted to be exposed to, and people you wanted to meet but never did.

RESPONDING TO JOB OFFERS

Following up with firms after you receive an offer is an extremely important part of the hiring process. You'd be amazed at the number of students who receive offers and never bother to communicate with the firm afterward. When you respond to offer letters, follow a few simple guidelines:

1. *Follow up with the firm immediately.* When you receive the offer letter in the mail, contact the recruiting coordinator or your contact just to let him or her know that you received the letter. Do this even if you plan to decline the offer.

2. *If you plan to decline the offer, do so as soon as possible.* There's no reason to hang on to an offer if you know you aren't going to accept it. This enables the firm to extend offers to others it may have on hold.

3. *There's no reason to wait to accept an offer, either.* If you know you want to accept an offer, do so immediately. This also helps the firm to plan, and it demonstrates your enthusiasm for the firm.

4. *Put your decision to decline or accept an offer in writing.* It makes good business sense to reiterate your final decision in writing. Attorneys as well as recruiters like to "dot their *i*'s and cross their *t*'s," and this is part of that process.

Keep in mind that how you react and respond to a job offer can reflect positively or negatively on you. Prolonging the agony of any kind of response gives the impression that you are indecisive. If you really are indecisive, ask for more time, but do so only once. There comes a time when you have to make a decision about where you want to work.

PART THREE

THE SUMMER PROGRAM

Obstacles are things a person sees when he takes his eyes off his goal.

—E. JOSEPH COSSMAN

11

HOW TO HAVE A
SUCCESSFUL SUMMER

"A resume tailor-made for a firm like yours that has a cookie-cutter
approach to hiring!"

Now that you have been through the grueling recruiting process and have
found a home for the summer, you are ready to jump on the law firm
bandwagon as a summer associate. There are worse ways to spend a summer.
My father always said that if he could be reincarnated, he wanted to be a
summer associate in his next life. The decadent summer programs of the
1980s may be gone, but being a summer associate, even today, remains an
educational and event-filled experience.

Once you have decided where to work for the summer, make an effort to
stay in touch with the firm during the winter and spring months. Contact the
firm every few months just to say hello, or if proximity allows, stop in and
meet the attorneys face-to-face. Your transition to summer associate will be
easier if you make a few friends before coming on board. The attorneys will
feel more comfortable with you, and you will feel more at ease with them.
The firm will also appreciate the effort you make to stay in touch, especially
if you are the only summer associate who has taken the trouble to do so.

MAKE YOUR TRANSITION TO
SUMMER ASSOCIATE SEAMLESS

Law students put tremendous pressure on themselves to be successful summer associates. But some students fail, not because they cannot do the work, but because they fail to make a seamless transition from law student to summer associate. Being able to do the work is imperative, but you also must "fit" into the firm and make a solid impression. Before becoming a summer associate, many students have little exposure to law firm culture. Students sometimes try too hard to fit in. They overcompensate for their shortcomings despite the fact that everyone has them. Be yourself, never forgetting that the firm hired you because they liked you. The following are some overlooked guidelines that should help you succeed as a summer associate. Some of this advice is the same as for first-year summer associates, but it is worth repeating:

1. *Ask and ask some more.* If you don't know how to do something, even the simplest task, ask. It's better to obtain guidance than to guess at how things might be done. Everyone, in any company, faces this problem when they start a new job. Don't photocopy a box of 200 documents just because you think the client might want it. Ask first. The client and the firm will appreciate your inquisitive mind.

2. *Treat the support staff with the respect they deserve.* In many firms, the support staff knows as much about the practice of law as experienced attorneys. Getting on their good side can only help you. You'll be amazed at what some of them know.

3. *Learn the politics early on.* Even the smallest firms are embroiled with office politics. Remain neutral at all times, but learn how the ball bounces in your court. Learn who the gossipers are, stay away from them, and avoid hearsay.

4. *Don't get in over your head.* If you're asked to do something that is too much for your level of experience, say so. Many attorneys will assume you know how to do what you are asked unless you tell them otherwise. It's harder to get out than to stay out.

5. *Don't compete with your classmates.* Nothing can ruin a summer program (for everyone) quicker than competing with your peers. Summer programs are not horse races. The students who fit in and can do the work should receive job offers. No one gets brownie points for one-upmanship.

6. *Quality is better than quantity.* Don't take on too many assignments so that you can't deliver the goods. No one is holding a bean counter, tallying each assignment. It is far better to complete a few really good pro-

jects than to produce folders of mediocre work. Everyone will remember the poor assignment you produced.

7. *Don't let yourself fall between the cracks.* Every summer there is always one student who tends to get lost and is less visible than the others. Make sure you stay afloat. If you are physically tucked away, out of the mainstream of firm activity, you may be forgotten. It is up to you not to let this happen.

8. *Don't become known only as a social or party animal.* There is ample opportunity during the summer program to kick up your heels and have a great time—and you should. But don't become known as the Holly Golightly of the summer program. Make sure the firm sees your serious side more often than your playful side.

9. *Establish multiple mentors—partners and associates.* Develop bonds with several attorneys over the summer. Too many students have been led astray by associates or partners who fed them incorrect information or were not liked by others in the firm. Since you won't know enough to decipher who the "in" and "out" people are, bond with several people just to be safe.

10. *Learn how to research before you become a summer associate.* Former summer associates often reveal that their initial research skills were less than satisfactory when they first became a summer associate. Many had to quickly come up to speed, spending much of their free time learning how to research. Take advantage of your law school resources prior to joining a firm for the summer. This includes becoming proficient on LEXIS and Westlaw before the summer program begins.

11. *Don't burn your bridges.* No matter how much you like or dislike your firm, maintain good relations. The legal community is just too small to make enemies or leave a black mark this early in your career. Trust me. As a good example of what not to do, consider the story of one summer associate who didn't like the firm he clerked for one summer. He collected business cards from the partners throughout the summer. At the end of the summer, before he left for school, he decided to visit a local "all men's club," where he proceeded to hand out the partners' business cards he had collected all summer. Needless to say, the partners were not amused. Fortunately for the firm, the local legal press failed to pick up the story. I hope this student never runs into any of those partners later in life.

EMILY POST, THE LAW STUDENT— SUMMER ASSOCIATE ETIQUETTE 101

Doing the legal work is often much easier than figuring out how to be socially and politically correct in a law firm, especially if you only have eight or ten weeks (or less) to make a positive impression. While the rules vary from firm to firm, big city to small town, east to west, and north to south, there are some general rules that you should follow, adapting them to your particular environment.

Dress for Success

Dressing for work is no different from dressing for interviews. The challenge is making that impression last for an entire summer. While your appearance alone won't make or break your chances of getting an offer unless you always appear slovenly, it's an important piece of the puzzle. It's easy to do this right.

1. *Arrive at work every day dressed and ready to go.* Don't commute in your jogging clothes, maintaining your closet on the back of your office door, making your transformation in your office to summer associate. Come to work ready to work. Put your makeup on or shave at home.
2. *Always look neat.* A slovenly appearance gives the impression that you may be sloppy in other areas of your life as well. Look as though you have your act together, even if you don't. This means taking care of the details that you may think others do not notice—some people will always take notice. Make sure your socks match. Shine your shoes. Wear clean and smooth panty hose. Shoes should match your outfit. Wear minimal and conservative jewelry. Keep your hair neatly cut. Wear clean ties, and keep a spare in your office in case the one you're wearing gets dirty. Your shirts should be pressed, preferably by a dry cleaner. And don't wear too much perfume or aftershave. Carry breath mints with you to avoid bad breath. The difference is in the details.
3. *Look well dressed.* You don't have to shop at Barney's or have a trust fund to look well dressed. Invest in a few good suits, and wear them repeatedly. No one is counting how many outfits you have or if you have worn that suit three times already this week. Look like a professional at all times. Women can wear dresses as well as suits. No one expects you to wear a navy blue suit to work every day.
4. *Follow your dress code at any events where firm members are present.* This includes Saturday afternoon baseball outings, sailing parties, or in-

formal cookouts at associates' homes. You should be as neat in your informal attire as in your weekday wardrobe. Try to be yourself in your dress habits, but if in doubt, opt for the conservative. Partners may not approve of earrings on men, microminis on women, or the grunge look. Leave these at home, and save them for time spent with your friends completely outside your work environment.

How to Address Higher-Ups

You should always know the proper way to address the more senior attorneys in a firm. While each firm is different and some are more formal than others, always assume that formality is the rule, not the exception. Address most attorneys by their last name until you are told otherwise. Associates will want to be called by their first names, as will many partners, but they will appreciate the respect shown to them.

Many firms now have various classes of attorneys (of counsel, staff attorney, local partner, etc.), and initially you may not know what these classes mean. There was a very influential former government official in one firm who was classified "Of Counsel," so a summer associate assumed that he was not as important as a partner. The student proceeded to call this attorney by his first name, joked with him, failing to treat him with the respect he would grant a partner. This display of disrespect really irritated the attorney, who was accustomed to being treated as a dignitary, and it left him with a sour first impression of the summer associate. Never assume anything when addressing other attorneys until you have all the facts. Even then, respect and courtesy never go out of style.

Get Involved in Firm Activities

One of the most important things you can do is to get involved in firm activities during the summer. Interest is the sincerest form of flattery. And attorneys think that students who are not involved are less interested than their more involved colleagues. While you don't have to go to every breakfast meeting, every training session, or every event a firm sponsors during the summer, you should make a conscious effort to get involved on a fairly regular basis, attending all major firm events. There are always some firm members who make note of who is and is not present, and you probably won't know who those people are.

If your firm has a summer sports league such as softball, volleyball, Frisbee, or golf, make an effort to join a team. While you don't have to be minor-league quality to participate, this is an excellent opportunity to mingle with people strictly on a social basis and get to know those attorneys you may not have the opportunity to work with. Informal team sports can be a lot of fun as well. Some firms also view sports as a way to see if you are a team player.

Don't Date Others in the Firm

In my opinion, summer associate dating is never a good idea. Believe it or not, there is often more interoffice romance going on during the summer than many think. Find others, outside the firm, to date during the summer. Don't mix your business and personal life while you are being evaluated for a future position. While I may sound old-fashioned, this practice leaves a negative impression. If you think you have met Mr. or Ms. Right during the summer, hold off until you complete your internship with the firm. Firms always seem to find out about interoffice dating, even if you think you are keeping it a secret. Just say no from the very beginning.

Keep a Positive Attitude

Some firms, especially in the large metropolitan areas, report that larger percentages of summer associates are coming into their firms with major attitude problems. For example, one firm recounted how several members of a recent summer class complained bitterly all summer, no matter what the firm did. They wanted to work for more partners. They wanted to be treated like associates instead of summer associates. They wanted to do different types of work than they were doing. Even though this group complained most of the summer, they managed to produce quality work. But you cannot imagine how relieved and happy the attorneys and the staff were when the summer program ended and Beavis and Butt-head went home. *Summer associate* was becoming a four-letter term in this law firm. Do not take the summer program concept for granted, and leave your complaining at home!

Act Interested in What You're Doing

Whether you're completing a work assignment, going to a trial with a partner, attending an administrative hearing, or having dinner with several associates, put up a positive front. Firms are reluctant to give offers to students they think will not accept them. Show enthusiasm, without going overboard, for what you are doing, even if you have to brush up on your acting skills.

Learning to get along with all types of people in an unfamiliar environment takes time and patience. Argumentative summer associates don't fare very well. Learn to adapt, even if it means holding on to your tongue. One summer associate who spent his entire summer at a major East Coast firm was so overbearing that when the attorneys saw him coming down the hall, they shut their doors and got on the phone. No one wanted anything to do with him. Needless to say, he had a very lonely summer and did not receive an offer, and even years later, no one was willing to give him a recommendation.

Have a Good Time, but Not Too Good a Time

You're supposed to enjoy your summer as well as work hard. But keep everything in moderation. The story of one student's escapades illustrates my point.

I'll call the star of my story William. William liked to party, and party he did. Unfortunately, the partners had no clue about William's primary goal for the summer—to have a good time. He was a first-year and decided early on that this summer he just wanted to have fun. William decided that he would worry about securing a job when he became a second-year student. One of William's anecdotes involved his house-sitting for a partner. He was supposed to take care of the partner's home for a week. The partner came home early to the horror of finding his wife's bronze statues lining the lawn (she was an artist) covered with the family underwear. When the partner made it to the office (luckily without having cardiac arrest), he found William smugly wearing one of his ties as well. William had borrowed the partner's clothes as well as his statues. Needless to say, William wasn't invited back the following summer, and if some of the members of the firm had gotten their way, he would have been banished from the state, not to mention the bar.

12

HOW SUMMER
PROGRAMS OPERATE

"Good luck with the interviews, but first familiarize yourself with this compendium
of topics and questions you must *avoid*."

Fitting into a firm is only half the battle. You must also learn how to master
the more technical aspects, the work assignments. You'll have an easier
time mastering the work if you first understand what firms expect from their
summer associates. What is important when you deliver an assignment?
How many assignments should you tackle at once? What types of mistakes
do firms find acceptable? How is work evaluated? I'll answer these questions
for you and give you some pointers on how to deliver the best work possible.
And again, the difference lies in the details.

HOW WORK IS HANDED OUT

Obtaining, handing out, and tracking work assignments in summer programs
are almost a full-time job in any summer program. Firms handle this process
differently, depending on their size, areas of practice, and management struc-
tures. You'll have little control on how work is handed out in your firm,
but it's helpful to understand how the work assignment process generally
works.

The Assignment Book Technique

Firms gather assignments, generally before the summer program starts, and place them in a binder, which is usually housed in either the recruiting coordinator's or hiring partner's office. When you need work, you select a project from the book. Sometimes the project will be selected for you, so you may have little say in which assignments you receive. If your firm uses this method, make sure you get a variety of assignments from as many areas of the firm as possible. Also make sure that at least some of your projects are billable.

The Rotation Program

Firms with distinct practice groups sometimes rotate summer associates through each practice area for a specific amount of time. Some firms will allow their summer associates to pick the areas they want to rotate through. If your firm uses this method, make sure that you find out early on how students are evaluated. A danger in adopting the rotation program is that the practice groups often want the same "star" students, leaving others out in the cold.

The "Vulture" or "Water Fountain" Method

The "vulture" or "water fountain" method is when the attorneys walk through the corridors and snatch up summer associates for projects. Once you catch on, if you have a lot of work, you never roam the halls. All firms practice this to a degree, but some are worse than others.

The "Land on Your Own Feet" Method

Some very independent and entrepreneurial firms tend to practice the "land on your own feet" method. Many firms will never admit to you that they expect you to gather at least some of your own work, but it's a wise idea to learn how to master the art of garnering your work assignments without the assistance of others in the firm. If you master this art, you'll never be without work.

DEVELOP GOOD WORK HABITS

Doing the work and learning the proper way to deliver the product are two completely different issues. It takes a while to adapt to a new working environment. Learning the proper procedures or channels of communication to get the work out takes time, which is in short supply during a summer internship.

Technology is a great leveler, and it plays a starring role in many law firms. Law students are often technologically more efficient than their associate and partner counterparts; and many come into firms frustrated by the lower technological standards. Each firm will be different in this regard. Some firms will give each summer associate his or her own computer, while others will not. It is not uncommon for students to bring their computers with them, especially laptops. Just be ready to adapt to whatever environment you find yourself in.

Working Smart Hints

Adapting to a work environment while working with multiple attorneys, each with a different working style, can be nerve-racking at best. The following are some helpful hints that may prove useful as you adapt to your new environment:

1. *Get a memo format.* Attorneys love to utilize hard copy memoranda, even when it would be easier to use e-mail. Therefore, many of your assignments will be delivered via written memo. Get a copy of the standard memo format in your firm during the first week, and learn to use it. Also, make sure you have copies of all of the formats if there is more than one.
2. *Keep copies of all your assignments.* Make a file, create a notebook, or keep a disk (whatever works for you) of all of your work assignments during the summer. That way, if anything is lost or misplaced, you have a backup copy. This also gives you a file of sample work products for future use if you need them. But don't wait until the end of the summer to start this project.
3. *Learn to juggle multiple assignments at once.* Summer associates come into a firm wanting to obtain an assignment, finish it, and then go on to the next one. Unfortunately, the real world does not work like this. You have to learn how to slay several dragons at one time, using the same sword. You'll probably struggle at first as you learn to do this, but to be successful you must be able to master this task. And the sooner you are able to work this way, the better.
4. *Keep up with your time in a timely manner.* You have to learn how to bill your time—a necessary evil ranked up there with getting a root canal. No one likes to keep track of his or her time, especially in tenth-of-an-hour increments. But learn to be efficient early on. Enter your time into the billing system weekly or even daily. Your billing partners will love you, and your secretary will love you even more.

5. *Never assume that you know the billing policies of clients.* When you receive an assignment from an attorney, ask if there are any billing policies you need to know about. Some clients have established specific billing guidelines, which you will not know about and the attorneys may forget to tell you.

6. *Get permission to bill Westlaw/LEXIS time before you start.* Computer research time is not free anymore. Just to be safe, get prior permission to bill computer research time to clients. Many summer associates have left firms with $1,000 Westlaw bills, unknown to the client, making many billing partners very unhappy. Get the green light on the front end, and be efficient when you work. Get the firm librarian to help you in the beginning as you learn to be an efficient online researcher.

7. *Stay in touch with attorneys who give you long-term work assignments.* You will probably receive a mix of short- and long-term assignments over the summer. There is always at least one summer associate who alienates a partner who gives out a long-term assignment, never hearing from that student again until the end of the summer. Make a weekly progress report to the attorney, indicating where you are with the project, even if you have to do this for the entire summer. Some attorneys believe in the "out of sight, out of mind" philosophy—if they don't hear from you, they think you aren't working on an assignment or aren't interested in it. Communication is key. Make sure you communicate frequently on the long projects.

8. *Become good friends with the librarian and the MIS director.* Despite what many senior partners think, a firm is helpless without these two people. They are invaluable resources for everyone in the firm. Get to know them well over the course of the summer.

9. *Ask for feedback.* Generally, attorneys are not good at giving feedback to summer associates, and therefore students are often disappointed with the amount of feedback they receive. Put the burden on yourself for obtaining comments on your work. No one will fault you for taking the initiative.

SUMMER ASSOCIATE EVALUATIONS

You should know, from the very beginning of your clerkship, how you'll be evaluated over the course of the summer. This knowledge should include who is involved in the evaluation process (i.e., which attorneys evaluate you), how often you'll be evaluated (once or twice during the summer or more), and what criteria will be used to evaluate you. Without this knowledge, you may not know what the firm is looking for in its future associates.

If possible, get the firm to show you a blank evaluation form. Keep in mind that all firms will have a different evaluation form.

In large firms, the evaluation process is often very structured, while in smaller firms, the process will probably be more informal and loosely designed, if it formally exists at all. While the procedures vary from firm to firm, I've outlined below how the process works in one large firm, which I'll call Smith & Jones.

General Evaluations

If you were working at Smith & Jones, you'd be evaluated twice during the summer (only once if you're there for half of the summer). You're apprised of the evaluation process during the orientation you receive during your first week. Each attorney in the firm is given the opportunity to evaluate every student by completing an evaluation form on each one or by giving feedback directly to a member of the recruiting committee. If an attorney chooses the latter method, his or her comments are recorded during the meeting. These two evaluations are general in nature. All evaluations are kept under lock and key by the recruiting coordinator. Summer associates are never allowed to review their evaluations.

The first evaluation, which usually takes place at the end of June, is intended to identify any major problem areas. Hopefully, if problems are identified at this early stage, they can be remedied. For example, a student might have an abrasive personality, which is offending firm members. Or a student might be treating the staff in a rude manner. Fortunately, negative evaluations are not the norm. At Smith & Jones, an associate and a partner from the recruiting committee sit down with the student and deliver the evaluation. This session can be as short as ten minutes, or if there are major problems, it can take hours. If problem areas are identified, a follow-up session is usually scheduled in a few weeks in an effort to remedy the situation.

The second evaluation, which is given at the end of the summer, acts as a "summary." By this time, firm members should have gotten to know you and your peers well enough to evaluate you. Attorneys are usually instructed to ask themselves, "Is this someone with whom I want to work? Do I like this summer associate? Does he or she possess the necessary criteria to be a successful attorney in this firm?" As you would expect, much more information is gathered during this evaluation. As during the midsummer evaluation, representatives from the recruiting committee meet with you and deliver the evaluation. This is usually done sometime during your last week at the firm.

Individual Work Evaluations

Separate from the overall evaluations are the individual work evaluations. These are just as important as the general evaluations. If you are able to do the work but can't "fit" into the firm, you probably don't have a future there. If everyone loves you, but you simply cannot do the work at the level required, then your offer potential is equally weak. Take a look at the sample work evaluation form below. One work evaluation form is completed by the assigning attorney for each project you complete.

Obviously, work evaluations are handled differently in different firms. At Smith & Jones, the recruiting coordinator keeps track of which assignments are given to each summer associate. She then contacts the assigning attorneys once the work is completed, attempting to obtain a completed evaluation form. She maintains contact with the attorneys until the evaluation is handed in. Once the evaluations are received, if there are any negative comments, she contacts the attorney for further feedback, attempting to identify any real problems. All work evaluations are kept under lock and key. Only members of the recruiting committee see the actual evaluations. The attorneys are more willing to write down information if they know that their audience is limited. The summer associates never see the completed evaluations on their work.

My experience has shown that students seem to be more concerned with the work evaluations than their overall evaluations. You should be equally concerned with both. While improving the quality of your work is easier to control, you don't want to end up in a firm that clashes with your personality type.

HIRING DECISIONS

There are many pieces to the puzzle that influences how firms make hiring decisions. While it's probably impossible for you to know what the pieces to that puzzle are for your particular firm, your best bet is to gain an overall knowledge of the factors that most firms have to deal with—factors such as law firm politics, law firm economics, and the size of the summer associate class, for example.

The Time Lag Factor

Consider the fact that second-year recruiting is done almost two years in advance. So much can change within a firm from the time that you are hired during the fall of your second year and the time that you report to work as an associate once you've completed law school. A partner with millions of dol-

BELL, BOOK & CANDLE
Washington, D.C.
SUMMER ASSOCIATE PROJECT EVALUATION
1994

PLEASE RETURN TO ANN OGBURN PROMPLY IN A SEALED ENVELOPE.

SUMMER ASSOCIATE: _____

CLIENT/NATURE OF CASE: _____

APPROXIMATE TIME SPENT ON PROJECT: _____

LEVEL OF DIFFICULTY (Circle One):   • **DIFFICULT**   • **MODERATE**   • **EASY**

RATING: (If a category does not apply, please indicate)

CATEGORY	Outstanding	Above Average	Average	Below Average
1. Research				
2. Analysis				
3. Organization				
4. Writing				
5. Ingenuity/Creativity				
6. Verbal Ability				
7. Motivation/Initiative				
8. Promptness				
9. Manner, Presence, & Poise				
10. Overall				

Comments: _____

_____

_____

Signed: _____   Date: _____

lars of portable business can leave a firm, a major client may go to another law firm, regulatory changes can dry up work in a particular area—these are just a few examples. And infighting and indecision can also have an adverse effect on hiring.

The Actual Hiring Decision

Firms decide to hire students in different ways. In most firms, the partners must vote on associate hiring decisions. This is often done after receiving recommendations from the recruiting committee and the wishes of certain practice or work groups. Large firms are sometimes organized along practice group lines, and hiring often follows this alignment. At Smith & Jones, for example, the trust and estates practice decides how many associates they want to hire for that practice, and the trust and estates partners actually determine which summer associates get hired for their practice. The method works for other departments in the firm as well.

Some large and medium-sized firms have a general rotation for the first year or two, and new associates are not assigned to a practice group until the end of the second year. Associates are hired as a "pool" based on the general projected needs of the firm. In small firms, the partners decide if they have the financial resources and the workload to hire additional associates.

PART FOUR

GETTING A JOB AS A THIRD-YEAR STUDENT

Experience is not what happens to you but what you make of what happens to you.

—Aldous Huxley

13

LAYING THE GROUNDWORK FOR FINDING A NEW ASSOCIATE POSITION

"Litigation is what I love! I've sued every one of my prior employers!"

It's not unusual in the current job market to be a third-year student without law firm job prospects by the time graduation rolls around. But don't despair and lose complete faith in your ability to find a position as a third-year student or beyond. Increasingly, many firms, especially the small ones, are waiting until after students take and pass the bar exam to hire new associates. This isn't great news if you have to foot the bill for the bar exam and review course and if you have the added anxiety of graduating from law school, heavily burdened with student loan debt, without a job.

The good news is that law firm positions do exist, but you might have to lower your expectations and look in places you probably haven't thought of to find them. You may find that locating a needle in a haystack isn't as difficult as you thought. Your road has gotten narrower and steeper, but with perseverance and some additional planning, you can locate legal employment, albeit maybe not the dream job you once envisioned, during or immediately after your third year of law school.

THE THIRD-YEAR RESUME

Your third-year resume shouldn't differ much from your first- and second-year versions. Obviously, you should include work and educational experience from your two previous summers and any recent academic honors you might have received. This information should easily fit on one page, unless you have significant work experience. Refer to the sample third-year resume on the following page.

How to Make Your Resume Look Good Despite Setbacks

A big dilemma for many students at this point in their job search is how to positively portray work experiences that didn't lead to job offers. If you received a job offer from a former summer employer, you should indicate that on your resume. And always include all of your past summer legal-related positions on your resume, even if you didn't receive job offers. Obviously, it's improper as well as misleading to omit pieces of your work history. A good recruiter will immediately look for gaps in your work history. Many firms make their new employees, including associates, sign a completed job application, testifying to the fact that their chronological work history has no omissions. But there is a delicate art to handling negative work situations, which anyone seeking employment should learn how to finesse.

Let's face it—it's not unusual in today's working world to have been fired, laid off, or simply not given a job offer. As devastating as any of these experiences can be, most people are able to turn a negative situation around and go on to bigger and better things. Mastering the art of making a bad situation sound good is difficult at best, but not impossible.

Here's list of helpful hints that can aid you in making yourself look good to a potential legal employer:

1. *Use only positive verbs and adjectives on your resume.* For example, don't include statements such as "Firm decided not to make offers to any members of the summer associate class," even if it's true. Instead, you would make no reference to receiving an offer, but you might include the fact that *your* brief was used in an important trial. You only want positive verbiage coming off your page. But also make sure you don't sound overly enthusiastic to the point of appearing desperate. Somewhere in between is a happy medium.
2. *Never say anything negative, in person or in writing, about a former employer, no matter how bad the experience.* The thinking is that if you'll say something negative about one employer, you'll say something bad about all of them, including future employers. Negative comments send

Third-Year Resume

William R. Evans
498 Avalon Road, Apartment 12
Gainesville, FL 32611
904-566-7861

Education

UNIVERSITY OF FLORIDA, J.D., expected 1996
GPA—3.0, estimated top 1/3
President, Environmental Law Society
First-Year Writing Instructor

WASHINGTON & LEE UNIVERSITY, Lexington, Va., B.A. History, 1992
GPA—3.2
Member, Varsity Tennis Team

Experience

Summer
1995

WESTON, HILL & NELSON
Philadelphia, Pennsylvania
Summer Associate
Worked primarily on litigation matters in insurance defense firm. Attended depositions and trials. Worked on briefs and memos for clients. Attended numerous trial technique training sessions.

Summer
1994

NATIONAL LEGAL WEEKLY
Washington, D.C.
Writer Intern
Interned at national legal weekly publication's main office. Worked with reporters in writing copy, proofreading, checking references, etc. Worked exclusively in the environmental and legislative areas.

1993–
1994

LEGAL AID SOCIETY OF GREATER TAMPA
Tampa, Florida
Paralegal/Law Clerk
Started as unpaid intern, performing general duties in nonprofit legal clinic. Promoted to paid staff member. Worked with clients, attended hearings, depositions, etc. Acted as receptionist, courier, clerk, paralegal, etc.

Summer of
1992

Traveled extensively in South America for three months in Chile, Argentina, Peru, Bolivia, Colombia. Wrote chapters on Peru and Bolivia for national travel guide. Also wrote travel stories for three local newspapers.

Interests/Skills

Familiar with Excel, Word, Lotus, and WordPerfect. Proficient on the Internet and Web. Tennis instructor. Interests include freelance writing, rugby, travel.

negative messages to the outside world. And people never forget your negative comments.

3. *Embellish your experience, and add it to your resume.* If you failed to obtain the summer job you wanted during your second summer, add to your resume by volunteering during the school year, or do something that will add to your experience. If nothing else, your work history will look better on paper. For example, if you're interested in litigation, volunteer at the local courthouse, work on litigation cases at the Legal Aid Society, or clerk for a judge during the school year. You may not have a job offer on your resume, but you've added other things.

4. *If your grades are less than stellar, leave them off.* If you have less than a 3.0 average (on a 4.0 scale) or are not in the top third of your class, omit your grade point average. But if there is a pattern to your grades— your grades have steadily improved since your first year, or you had a good average except for the one semester in which your favorite uncle passed away—include a transcript with your resume, and note the pattern in your cover letter.

5. *Attempt to differentiate yourself.* At this point in your law school career, you have the ability to differentiate yourself from the rest of your peers. You're the one who held all the offices in law school, a born leader. Every activity you participated in involved your interest in environmental law. You're a well-known equestrian in your spare time, or you have a fabulous golf handicap. Make it appear that you are different from your classmates by bragging about yourself and your accomplishments just a little bit. Don't be dishonest, but bring your strong points to the surface for the reader to see.

REFERENCES

As a third-year student without a job, it's probably best not to include references on your resume. If you don't have a position at this point, you should control who calls whom during this process. You must make sure that all reference checks come out positive, leaving no trace of doubt in any employer's mind. This is absolutely critical at this stage of your job search.

Whom should you use as a reference? Law firms will want to talk to someone who knows your legal skills outside of the academic law school environment. A seasoned recruiting coordinator will ask you for individuals from your two or three most recent jobs. You can include professors, but not to the exclusion of practicing attorneys or judges. Someone should definitely be on your list who worked with you in your most recent job, even if that includes the firm that declined to make you an offer.

When you select one or two attorneys from your last position, talk to them before you give their name out as a reference. Make sure that their stories are the same, including why you didn't get an offer from the firm. Since most people are reluctant to give bad references in our litigious society, it's unlikely that anyone will say anything negative about you. But one of the biggest red flags to a seasoned recruiting professional is when someone is too quick to tell you that they can't say anything or when stories are inconsistent. And very often you can convince people to talk positively about someone "off the record," even if firm policy is to do otherwise.

As an example of a "red flag," I once checked the references of a woman who had worked for several excellent law firms but never for any length of time. When checking her references, I could hardly get the woman's name out of my mouth when the person on the other end said that he or she could not tell me anything about the candidate. Immediately, I knew something was wrong. Finally, I was able to determine that this woman had numerous personal problems that would make her an undesirable candidate. I inferred from the tone of the conversation that something was wrong, even though nothing negative was ever said.

THE COVER LETTER

The wording and overall message in the cover letter are critical in the case of the third-year student without a job offer. The first question any law firm is going to ask is "Why is this person still looking for a job?" You must learn to be savvy without crossing the boundary of misrepresenting your situation. Your goal is to interest the firm enough so that the negative obstacles can be overcome. Many recruiting professionals indicate that they like to get the overall picture of a candidate by reading the cover letter. Since most of us don't write like Ernest Hemingway, it can be extremely difficult to create such an impression in a few short paragraphs. With some work, however, it can be done. Once you take the time to create a really good cover letter, use it over and over, making minor alterations for different positions. Refer to the ones you used as a first- and second-year student as well.

Stress the Positive

Your primary goal is to stress the positive. You don't have to mention why you are in the market for a job if you leave little doubt in the reader's mind that you are a viable candidate—or at least one worth inquiring about.

For example, you can indicate that while you worked for a firm last year in New Orleans, your focus now is only on the East Coast because your

Third-Year Cover Letter

498 Avalon Road, Apartment 12
Gainesville, FL 32611
904-566-7831

November 15, 1995

Ms. Elizabeth R. Nelson
Recruiting Director
Truluck & Davis
30 West Hilltop Street
Chicago, IL 60603

Dear Ms. Nelson:

I recently saw your posting for an entry-level litigation associate in my law school placement bulletin. My resume is attached for your review and consideration. As a third-year completing my studies at the University of Florida, I am eager to relocate to the Chicago area, where my fiancee has entered graduate school.

Litigation and environmental law are the two areas in which I am interested. The amount of litigation experience that I possess is atypical for a third-year law student. While clerking in a litigation boutique firm in Philadelphia last summer, I gained hands-on experience with two well-known litigators. In addition, I worked in the Legal Aid Society in Tampa for two years before attending law school, which gave me a unique perspective into the court system.

My job search now focuses exclusively on the Chicago area because of my fiancee's situation. I will be in Chicago starting in mid-December through the end of January and would like very much to talk with you during that time. I will contact you in a few weeks, in the hopes that a mutually convenient time for an interview can be arranged.

In the interim, I can be reached at the above address and phone number. Thank you, in advance, for your consideration, and I look forward to talking with you.

Sincerely,

William R. Evans

fiance was accepted to medical schools only in the East. Or you can state that your fiance has entered graduate school in Los Angeles, which has made it necessary for you to work in that area. You can come up with numerous reasons to be on the job market at this stage without lying about your situation or misrepresenting yourself. Just don't give the reader the impression that you were passed over, even if you were. Reread your cover letter, and ask yourself if it leaves you with a positive impression. Have several of your friends do the same. Just remember that no one, especially attorneys, wants to be involved with someone who leaves you with a bad taste in your mouth. Review the sample cover letter on the previous page, and note how it stresses the positive, even in a negative situation.

CHECKING GRADES AND BAR RESULTS

Another common practice in law firms (and in corporate America as well) is the verification of law school graduation, grades, and bar results. It has become a routine practice for firms to request a final official law school transcript from the registrar's office and evidence of bar membership, if applicable. If you change law firms as a lateral, expect to be asked again for this information. Firms are forced to demand this evidence, as "fake" lawyers have been hired who never completed law school and even passed a bar exam. You can speed up the process by having these needed materials on hand at all times.

14

WHERE TO LOOK
FOR NEW
ASSOCIATE POSITIONS

"All law firms make mistakes now and again. Ours was hiring you."

The key to finding a position as a third-year student is to determine which firms are hiring. Some firms hire new associates all of the time, while others hire only once in a ten-year period. Your job is to keep moving and to find and target the firms that are hiring now. Your best bet is to stay away from the large firms (firms with over 75 to 100 attorneys) and concentrate on the smaller firms, unless you can get on-campus interviews. The very large firms report that they are increasingly hiring fewer third-year students. It's common knowledge in the industry that large firms are filling their needs more and more out of summer programs.

The statistics clearly paint this picture. According to data from the National Association for Law Placement for the class of 1993, two-thirds of the jobs in firms of 11 to 25 people were obtained before graduation. This compares with 85.4 percent and 89.4 percent of jobs obtained before graduation in firms of 51 to 100 and more than 100 attorneys, respectively. At the smaller firms, one in five jobs were obtained after graduation but before bar results, and about one in seven (13.8%) were obtained after bar results. Over half of jobs (52.2%) in very small firms were obtained after graduation, and nearly one-quarter were obtained after bar results. It was more typical for a job to be obtained after graduation in a small firm (25 attorneys or less) than for one to be obtained before graduation in a firm of more than 100 attorneys.

READ THE NEWSPAPERS

Law students are typically avid readers. But they often fail to utilize their reading skills outside of an academic environment. The newspaper is full of information beyond the employment advertisements that can steer to job leads. Educating yourself about the market **in general** is vital to your job search at this point. Remember, looking for a needle in a haystack isn't easy.

What to Look For

Take the time to read all kinds of newspapers—from *The Wall Street Journal* and *National Law Journal* to your local newspaper in your hometown. There are all kinds of useful information available that you probably never thought of. Remember, you're looking for information that can lead you to more information—and ultimately to identifying the needs that a firm or company may have. Your possibilities with these sources are infinite.

In Smaller Newspapers

Here are some of the things you should look for in smaller-circulation, local newspapers:

- Law firms that have promoted associates to partners (which can create an opening) or partners who have moved from one firm to another.
- Judges who have recently been appointed (which can create an opening in the judge's former firm).
- Lawsuits that have been filed by local companies. Find out who their counsel is, and contact them directly.
- Firms that appear to be in the news often. They either have a lot of work or a good marketing department, or both.

In Larger Newspapers and the Legal Press

In larger newspapers and the legal press, look for the following kinds of information:

- Companies that are going public. Find out who their legal counsel is, and contact them.
- The stock market pages. Which companies are experiencing exponential growth? Which firms do these companies employ?
- Law firm mergers. While downsizing often accompanies mergers, they also create spin-off firms. Find out if spin-offs were created and if needs exist in these new, small firms.
- Keep an eye out for influential government and political figures who join firms. While often there is a lag time before these players generate large amounts of work (and the need for new associates), it may be wise to keep tabs on these firms and their future needs.

SMALL AND MEDIUM-SIZED FIRMS

Small and medium-sized firms primarily hire when business increases and to replace departing attorneys. Usually, their needs are so small that predicting these events in advance is impossible. Also, they don't have the economic ability to hire associates who won't be fully utilized. Some firms will require that an associate be licensed (in the right jurisdiction) and ready to start work when the interview process gets under way. When they need someone, they need someone who is available almost immediately in many cases. Sometimes, though, they'll hire new associates right before the bar exam and will sometimes assist you in paying the bar fees.

Often the smaller firms fill their positions through word of mouth and professional recommendations. Sometimes the firms contact local law schools for resumes. This is where your networking skills come into play. If you have established a network in a particular area as we discussed in Chapters 2 and 8, chances are you'll find out about these openings. And occasionally these jobs appear in newspapers. Even the small firms report, however, that they often receive hundreds of resumes for just one position.

LARGE FIRMS

Large firms sometimes hire third-year students to fill needs not met from the summer program or because of attrition at or near the entry-level stage. If a large percentage of a firm's summer associates accept judicial clerkships, there may also be a need to hire third-year students. Many large firms are able to assess and identify these needs before the fall interviewing season gets under way. Often, these needs are targeted to specific work groups. For example, the labor department may need two new associates, but only one person from the summer program was interested in labor.

Openings in Specific Practice Areas

This creates a caveat for the third-year student interviewing on-campus with large firms. The student may be interested in doing corporate or tax work, but the firm's only opening is in the labor department. By stating your interests, you eliminate your chances of getting an in-house interview with the firm. Be honest with yourself, and think long-term. If you do not want to do labor work, save yourself and the firm a lot of time and expense by eliminating yourself from the start. In the long run, you will not be happy working in an area that does not interest you just to get your foot in the door.

Often, when firms have specific needs, they look for course work or work experience on a resume that may indicate an interest in a particular area. Professors are often contacted as well for recommendations. Firms also post jobs in schools that are known for their specific expertise. For example, NYU and Florida have strong tax programs, and Franklin Pierce and George Washington are known for their intellectual property programs. Many firms with needs in specific areas will concentrate on certain schools to fill these needs.

You Need Previous Summer Associate Experience

Large firms almost *always* look for second-year summer clerkships on third-year resumes. Many recruiting coordinators state that it is a huge red flag to see a student who failed to work in a law firm as a second-year who is attempting to work in a firm after graduation. Many will not consider, under any circumstances, a third-year student who has not already clerked for a law firm.

Some large firms also will not consider third-year students who didn't receive an offer from the previous summer's law firm employer. While this practice seems very unfair, some firms will not budge from this criterion. The good news is that there are firms that will consider students who did not receive offers. There are numerous good reasons why even very strong students do not receive summer job offers. Some well-known firms have hired such students with great success. If you are in this boat, save yourself some valuable time, and determine from the very beginning which firms have adopted this practice.

STAFF ATTORNEY POSITIONS

Another option is to work in a firm as a "staff attorney." My definition of a staff attorney is an individual who is hired by a firm for a non-partnership-track position. Firms may use the term "staff attorney" to denote different employment arrangements, so if you are considering a staff attorney position, always ask the firm to define the concept in their own terms.

Why Firms Hire Staff Attorneys

Firms hire staff attorneys for different reasons. If you're considering a staff attorney position, make sure you understand the firm's philosophy behind the practice, including the economic implications. Following are instances when it makes good sense to hire staff attorneys rather than regular "on-track" associates:

1. *To staff areas that may not be lucrative enough to warrant hiring an on-track associate.* For example, one large regional firm has a collections practice, which exists only because several of the firm's valuable clients want and need this service. The collections practice isn't a moneymaking area for the firm—if it covers its expenses, the firm is happy. The only reason the firm maintains the practice is because some very valuable clients need and want the service. It doesn't make sense for the firm to put on-track attorneys in a practice that is unlikely to generate enough revenue to support an income partner and regular associates. But this practice area employs several associates who like their work, make good incomes, and don't have the stress of wondering whether they're going to make partner or not.

2. *To fill long-term temporary needs.* Some cases need additional manpower for long periods of time. Large litigation cases often present the dilemma of requiring more associates for periods of two to three years. Hiring staff attorneys provides an excellent solution to this problem.

How Firms Hire Staff Attorneys

Firms hire staff attorneys through newspaper and legal publication advertisements, through advertisements in placement offices, through word of mouth, and through personnel agencies. Usually you have to go through the normal recruiting process in firms to secure staff attorney positions. Academic credentials and previous work experience are criteria for these positions, but firms are far more lenient when they hire staff attorneys. But keep in mind that there is an academic level that some firms will never drop below, no matter what. You should be realistic about your chances of getting even a staff attorney position in a large firm if your grades are low or if you attended a relatively unknown law school.

Salary and Benefits

The salary arrangements for staff attorneys vary among firms. You should expect that the salaries for entry-level staff attorney positions are lower than those of regular on-track associates. Some firms even pay staff attorneys by the hour. But when comparing staff attorney salaries to regular associate rates, keep in mind the fact that staff attorneys are less likely to put in the large amounts of overtime that the regular associates are expected to work. In that regard, staff attorney positions can be a good value for the staff associate. And you don't have the headaches and stress associated with being an on-track associate.

Many staff attorneys also receive regular benefits if they are employed for at least six months to a year and work full-time hours. Obviously, benefits vary among firms, but if you are considered a "nontemporary" employee, you'll more than likely receive health benefits and paid vacation and holidays. But never assume that you'll receive benefits. Always ask firms what perks you would receive if hired as a staff attorney.

TEMPORARY POSITIONS

Temporary attorneys are hired, often through placement agencies or temporary agencies, to fill an immediate need in a firm. Unlike staff attorneys, temporary attorneys don't receive benefits and usually remain on the personnel agency's, not the law firm's, payroll. Temporary positions are an excellent way to get your foot in the door or to gain valuable experience that will, at the very least, enhance your resume and pay your bills.

In the large metropolitan areas, there are temporary firms that specialize in the legal industry. In less urban areas, consider going through a general temporary agency that does business with law firms. These firms pay you an hourly wage, marking up your rate to the law firm to make a profit. Taxes are withheld from your check, so you don't have to worry about working as an independent contractor, which can be a hassle when filing your income taxes.

One recent law school graduate found a very good temporary position at a well-known firm through a temporary legal agency in Washington, D.C., paying him $20 an hour, even though the average temporary jobs for entry-level attorneys were paying $12 an hour. He finds the work very challenging, and the firm has committed to keeping him employed for at least nine months, perhaps even longer. He's gaining excellent experience that will look good on his resume, at the very least.

Legal temporary agencies also report that some law firms are hiring temporary associates at all levels in order to try them out before hiring. As it's becoming extremely difficult to terminate individuals in our litigious society, hiring "temp to perm" is an excellent alternative. Corporate America has been using this vehicle for years.

Some law firms sometimes hire their temporary and staff attorneys as regular associates after they have been on the job and have performed extremely well. Usually the firms aren't looking to hire associates through these vehicles, but occasionally they find an exceptional individual who would probably have been overlooked during the regular recruiting process. This isn't the norm, and you shouldn't anticipate getting into a firm this way, but occasionally this does happen.

OTHER OPTIONS

As you probably know by now, searching for a job is full-time employment in itself. But if you've been diligently looking for employment and have not been able to find it by this stage, then it may make sense, both economically and for your self-esteem, to begin looking for work in other areas. And for many, the money runs out sooner rather than later. The good news is that you still have options.

Here are some other roads you may want to consider:

1. *Try temporary employment, not necessarily in a law firm.* This may not be ideal, and the pay is low, but working as a temporary employee helps pay the bills, gets you out into the working world, and may open some doors for you. Try to work for an agency that will place you in a law firm. Many larger firms will not hire law school grads for temporary positions because they realize that you are just trying to get your foot in the door, but others will. You never know what types of connections and contacts you may make once out in the working world.

2. *Try to get a clerkship outside of a law firm.* You may be able to gain some valuable experience working outside of a law firm that a law firm may find very attractive. For example, gaining legislative experience in Washington can be useful for certain law firms. Working for a high-tech company may appeal to a law firm that has many clients in that area. Working in a financial environment may be helpful if you want to do corporate work. Be creative and open-minded.

3. *Work for the government.* Working for the government may be very difficult in an age of government downsizing, but it may still be an option for you. There are government positions that law firms find very attractive. Positions at agencies such as the Securities and Exchange Commission, the Commodities Futures Trading Commission, the Commerce Department, the Internal Revenue Service, and the Treasury Department are very appealing to law firms, just to name a few. This may be your ticket, but you may have to wait a few years to enter a firm.

4. *Find a position outside of a law firm while you continue your job search.* This option tends to rear its head once the bank account runs dry. Out of economic necessity, you may have to find employment elsewhere. If you take this route, make sure you schedule time each week to continue your law firm job search.

5. *Open your own firm.* This is an expensive and scary option, but many people decide to hang their own shingle. Jay Foonberg, a solo practitioner and frequent public speaker, has an excellent book on this subject, which is published by the American Bar Association. If you are considering this option, read Foonberg's book first, and talk to a few solo practitioners before you make this commitment.

JUDICIAL CLERKSHIPS

Many students decide to accept judicial clerkships before going to work in a law firm. While there are considerations such as salary, staying out of the law firm market for another year or two, and the ability to get a clerkship, especially in the location you want, I've never heard anyone say that accepting a judicial clerkship was anything but an excellent decision.

Law firms almost always review judicial clerkships in a positive light, and most law firms want to hire former judicial clerks. Some firms have specific criteria when hiring judicial clerks, such as they hire only from certain courts or they prefer to hire individuals who clerk for judges in jurisdictions in which they regularly practice. But the majority of judicial clerks end up finding positions they are happy with.

Firms often opt to hire judicial clerks who were former summer associates instead of "cold" judicial clerks, unless the clerk has an exceptional law school record. Some firms will hold open slots for clerks who were summer associates, even for several years if they want the candidate badly enough. One firm held a position open for three years for a candidate who obtained a master's degree and then clerked for a judge!

Maintain Your Law Firm Connections

If you're planning to accept a judicial clerkship, you should maintain contact with the firms that you clerked for during the summer or with other firms you're interested in until you receive a job offer. Once you accept an offer with a firm, make an attempt to stay in contact with them until you report to work. This can be difficult if it's going to be two or even three years before you join the firm, but remaining in close contact can only help you.

Salary and Track-to-Partnership Issues

Firms differ tremendously on their policies of granting salary and track-to-partnership credit for judicial clerks. I think that most firms give judicial clerks at minimum one year of salary and partnership credit for clerkships, and some, but not all, will give you two years credit for two-year clerkships. If this is a big issue for you, find out on the front end what a firm's policy is regarding time and salary credit for clerkships.

The more prestigious the clerkship, the more bargaining power you're going to have. Those who manage to get a supreme court or appeals court clerkship can literally write their own tickets. Supreme court clerks get huge signing bonuses, often several years of partnership and salary credit, and are vigorously sought after.

One dilemma that firms are faced with is the economic impact of granting years of salary and partnership credit to incoming associates who have completed judicial clerkships. Students often have trouble understanding the roles economics play in firms. Billing rates are tied to salaries, rates are connected to the level and amount of work an associate receives, and the amount of work an associate completes is tied to how profitable he or she will be in the end.

As an example, if an associate is being paid $70,000, a common formula is to drop the last three zeros and bill the associate at a rate that is two and a half times that amount, or $175 per hour. If a new associate comes in and is being paid as a third-year associate from day one, his or her billing rate will more than likely reflect that. So you may find yourself as a new associate with a high salary and billing rate, with little work and even less law firm experience. And clients, in today's legal climate, are refusing to pay high rates for inexperienced associates. So don't negotiate too high or bite off more than you can chew, or you may eventually find yourself without a job.

PART FIVE

CHANGING JOBS AS A PRACTICING ATTORNEY—THE LATERAL JOB SEARCH

Ability is what you're capable of doing. Motivation determines what you do. Attitude determines how well you do it.

—LOU HOLTZ

15

GENERAL RULES FOR LATERAL HIRING

"I'm Mrs. Minnik's counsel. We're looking forward to reviewing your salary
and benefits package for her summer associate program at your firm."

In the turbulent job market of the 1990s, lateral hiring has become a common phenomenon in law firm circles. "Cherry picking," or hiring experienced lawyers with a solid book of portable business away from the competition, once sneered upon by law firms, now happens every day. Associates, with little loyalty to firms that cannot or will not wave the carrot of partnership in front of their noses, now regularly move from firm to firm, looking for a kinder and gentler lifestyle, more interesting work, better chances of making partner, or more money. In fact, it is becoming increasingly rare for attorneys to spend their careers under the roof of one law firm. It's safer now to view your job as a long-term project, instead of anticipating spending your career in one place anymore.

But how do you know when the time is right to make a lateral move? And how often can you change firms in the current legal market without blemishing your record? What do firms look for when they hire lateral candidates? And what can you, as an associate or partner, do to improve your chances of finding a better position in the lateral job market?

FIRM EXPERIENCE OR THE RIGHT CONNECTIONS

As a general rule, if you weren't able to break into the law firm market as a student, chances are slim that you can do so as a lateral attorney, unless you have a large book of portable business or extremely influential connections that may be useful to law firms. Unfortunately, most of us do not possess these connections. Be extremely realistic about how valuable your work experience may be to law firms.

One firm, for example, hired the former general counsel from a very influential government agency. He had no previous law firm experience and no portable business, but his experience and connections were valuable to law firms and their clients. However, as a rule, large law firms almost always look for previous law firm experience in their lateral attorney candidates. As one experienced recruiting coordinator states, "99.9 percent of lateral candidates need prior law firm experience." Defying the odds is not impossible, but extremely difficult, even under the best circumstances.

COMMON MISTAKES LATERALS MAKE PRIOR TO CHANGING JOBS

There are some common recruiting-related mistakes that associates make that make it more difficult to change jobs as a lateral attorney. If you have some insight early in your career, you can avoid these pitfalls, making lateral changes later much easier.

Failure to Focus on a Specialty Early in Your Career

One of the most common mistakes associates make is their failure to focus on an area of practice or specialty early in their career. By the end of your third year in a firm, you should narrow your focus to one or two practice areas. Otherwise, you may limit your marketability to other law firms. Keep in mind that if a firm has to retrain you in an area from the ground up, it's often more economical to hire an entry-level associate and pay him $70,000 than to retrain you, a third-year who's already earning a much higher salary.

Law firms also have their own way of doing things, and retraining is not always a welcome option. Retraining is often less attractive than hiring a "fresh" associate who hasn't been procedurally trained by another law firm. By the end of your third year in a law firm, you should be happy with your area of practice, or you should be willing to start closer to the bottom of the ladder in terms of salary and time credit in order to reinvent the wheel in another firm. In the current economic climate, clients have limited tolerance and pocketbooks for footing the bill for training associates. This is also why associates who have spent two years in a rotation program in a large firm, without specializing, sometimes have a tough time in the lateral job market unless their credentials are amazing.

If your specialty is administrative or regulatory in nature, you should have the beginnings of a subspecialty by the end of your third year. As an example, you might decide to specialize in regulatory matters in areas such as trade, tax, communications, or finance. Specific legal or nonlegal experience at agencies such as the Securities and Exchange Commission, the Federal Communications Commission, the Internal Revenue Service, or the Commodities Future Trading Commission is often useful to many law firms.

THE IDEAL TIME TO MAKE A MOVE

The ideal time for an associate to make a move is around the third year. This isn't set in stone, but this is the time frame commonly reported by experienced legal recruiting personnel. By this point, you aren't senior enough to create track-to-partnership problems, but you are senior enough to possess a solid foundation from which to work in another firm. By this time, you have skills that are useful to other law firms.

Don't Move Too Soon

While year three is an ideal time to change jobs, be careful not to make a lateral move too soon in your career. Firms may query when you move early on in your career. If you've only been with a firm for a year and want to move other than for reasons created by a second party (spouse relocation, for example) or for personal matters not related to your professional development, recruiting professionals may automatically question your judgment and performance in your current firm, regardless of your credentials. Firms want to know why you are moving after only months on the job. In these situations, recruiting coordinators often assume the negative until further investigation.

The following sorts of questions may immediately surface, and the interviewing firm will want answers:

- Did you fail to do enough due diligence on your current firm before you accepted the job offer? (This may demonstrate a lack of attention to detail or the fault of looking before leaping.)
- Are you a "whiner" who will never be happy in any firm?
- Are you the type of associate who gets "bored" and has to change firms every year or so?

- Is your work unsatisfactory so that you are being asked to leave?
- Do you have a major personality flaw and cannot get along with anyone?

These types of questions routinely come to the surface in recruiting professionals' minds in any type of service-based business, so do not be offended by their negative tone. As a potential lateral candidate, you need to understand what you are up against and the types of questions to which you will be subjected during the recruiting process. The more experience you have, the more difficult the recruiting process tends to be, the tougher the questions get, and the longer the process takes, so you've got to be prepared.

Don't Wait Too Long, Either

But don't wait too long to make your move, either. As you invest more time in a firm and move closer to partnership consideration, you're put under the microscope more often. Firms need time, often several years, to give their associates a good look before they decide if they're partnership material or not. And the economics of making a move in your later associate years often make moving around from firm to firm very difficult. I'll discuss the economics of lateral moves in Chapter 19.

SELECT THE RIGHT FIRMS BEFORE YOU BEGIN YOUR SEARCH

You probably thought that once you graduated from law school, passed the bar exam, and studied for an LL.M. degree at night, you would never have to contemplate doing legal homework ever again. Wrong on all accounts. As we discussed in Chapter 4, doing your homework is an integral part of a successful job search at any level. There are no shortcuts no matter who you are and what credentials and experience you may have. I've seen too many associates jump from one ship to another, creating more problems for themselves in their second law firm than in their first one, making the exact same mistakes, only because they failed to take the time to evaluate their current and future situations and find the firm that filled their needs.

How to Select Firms

How do you go about targeting and selecting the right law firm as a lateral candidate? It's not always an easy assignment, but the time spent is clearly worthwhile.

Determine what attributes you find attractive in your current firm and what aspects of your current job you find unattractive or unsettling. Even if you are happy where you are and your personal circumstances are forcing you to relocate, this exercise won't be in vain. Again, the adage "Know thyself" is critical to your finding the position that will satisfy your needs and challenge you professionally. This exercise helps you to understand which attributes you deem important in any law firm.

Make two lists, indicating the positive and negative attributes of your current law firm. Often, if you don't take the time to jot down the issues and actually see them written down on paper, it is difficult to visualize them clearly. After composing your lists, put them down for a few days, picking them up again after the dust has settled, ensuring that your ideas and feelings do not change over time. Therefore, it may take you a few weeks to finalize this exercise. You should reach a point where your lists don't change from one review to the next. Your list might look like the following:

Positive Attributes—Bell, Book & Candle

- Genuinely like most of the associates and partners
- Stability in staff
- Beautiful, modern offices in a convenient location
- Stable firm, well capitalized
- Solid firm management with strong financial executive
- Strong computer system, ahead of technology curve for a law firm
- Diverse attorney staff
- Community-oriented mentality
- Commitment to pro bono work

Negative Attributes—Bell, Book & Candle

- Too much internal competition in certain practice areas
- Partnership track too long
- Two tiers for partners
- Not marketing-oriented—need to spend more time and money on marketing
- Too much revenue generated by two or three large clients
- Staff gets away with too much—poor management in the human resources area
- Salary and benefits a little behind the market

When you begin interviewing with other firms, make a list of the attributes that you absolutely need your next employer to have and those that you absolutely will not tolerate. As you interview with these firms, determine which ones possess the attributes on your positive list. Eliminate those firms that do not stack up to your established criteria.

How It Really Works

To demonstrate how helpful this exercise can be, look what one associate discovered once he wrote down what was important to him. He was considering relocating from New York to Atlanta, after hearing so many great things about the great quality of life and friendly people in Atlanta. A friend convinced him to put down on paper the positive and negative aspects of his impending relocation. Once he completed this exercise, over a period of weeks, continually reviewing the positive and negative aspects of his choices on a printed page, he realized that he was much better off remaining in New York, that Atlanta did not offer him the attributes he discovered were important to him in a new firm. He decided to change firms, not location, remaining in New York, and is now much happier in his legal career.

While the purpose of this section is not to determine what color your parachute might be, performing this kind of internal due diligence is an integral part of any successful job search in any field of work. As you move up the ladder of experience in your legal career, this exercise becomes easier, but your universe of options gets smaller.

16

MARKETING YOURSELF AS A LATERAL ASSOCIATE

"How quickly can you switch over from Super Mario Brothers to LEXIS?"

Once you leave the cradle of law school and work as an attorney for a few years, you no longer have the unlimited time and access to your law school placement office you once did. Nor do you have the benefit of participating in the on-campus interview process when searching for a new position. While most schools offer limited placement services to alumnae, their first priority is placing their law students. And the myth exists, which has been perpetuated in recent years, that experienced attorneys should also be experienced in searching for a job. While legal search firms successfully assist many individuals in finding new positions, if you trod down this path for even a short distance, you'll quickly discover, as many law students do, that in many instances no one can find you a job for you better than you can. Finding a job is essentially your own responsibility. Your ability to successfully market yourself is a vital component of the legal job search.

Learning how to market yourself as an experienced attorney to potential employers, once you have handpicked the right firms, is easier for some than for others. The key, as we discussed in Chapter 4, is to know what you're looking for before you begin the process and to take the time to perform law firm due diligence before you start making phone calls and mailing your resume to potential employers.

Performing due diligence at this stage should be much easier as an experienced attorney, even if you have limited legal work experience, simply because you have more contacts in the industry. Once you've selected your geographic market, contact your peers and acquaintances. Find out which firms can offer you what you are looking for. Which firms have the clients you want to work for? Which firms offer sane lifestyles for their attorneys? Of all of your friends and acquaintances, which ones really enjoy their work? Take time to ask these types of questions and find the answers, off the record, **before** you jump into the job market.

USING LEGAL SEARCH FIRMS

Many experienced attorneys depend on legal search firms or "headhunters," as they are often affectionately known, to help them locate new positions. If you have worked in a law firm for very long, you probably have received cold calls from legal search consultants looking for attorneys to fill positions in other law firms. I'm sure that there are thousands of satisfied attorneys who have obtained positions with the assistance of a headhunter. But there is more to this animal than first meets the eye. You should understand how legal search consultants work. Knowledge is vital, especially when dealing with an industry that thrives on recruiting legal talent from one firm and offering it to another for a fee.

Search Firm Databases

Established legal search firms possess large databases of information on attorneys in law firms in a particular market or markets. An established firm knows who does what in which firm, and they are familiar with the "culture" of particular firms. They obtain this information by researching and working with firms and their attorneys, often over a period of many years. When they receive a job order from a firm for a specific position, they often already know where that talent exists. Once they identify where the talent is, they begin making cold calls to attorneys, attempting to find someone who may be willing to consider the position. Or they may have attorneys in their databases just waiting to locate the right opportunity. As scary as it may sound, they often know a lot about you before they make that phone call. But you should also be flattered that, in a tight job market, someone else may be interested in your talents and abilities.

How They Get Paid

Sometimes legal search firms are retained by a law firm to fill a specific position, earning a fee even if a suitable candidate isn't found. And sometimes they recruit attorneys, not knowing if there is another firm who can really use them. Their motivation may not necessarily be to find you the most suitable position, but to locate and place you in **any** position, so they can earn a fee. Their loyalty probably is to whomever is paying them—in this case, the law firm. But at the same time, if they place you in a position that isn't suitable for you, rest assured that the firm will be calling them, wanting their placement fee back, if you decide to leave within a short period of time—usually six months.

The fees that law firms pay legal search firms are substantial. Usually, they range from 20 to 30 percent of the attorney's gross salary for the first year they are employed at the new firm. Sometimes this figure will include bonuses. You can see that law firms are paying big bucks for exceptional legal talent or to fill holes that must be filled immediately.

I'm not trying to make headhunters appear as nasty villains whose only motivation is to make money. There are many reputable legal search consultants who have built fine reputations for themselves and who know the legal job market better than anyone else. And many headhunters make salaries that would be the envy of successful partners. Just understand how this process works before you get involved in it.

Select a Reputable Search Firm

If you decide to utilize the services of a legal search firm, take the time to research the legal search firm market in the area where you are interested in working. Randomly selecting any firm without checking references is just asking for trouble. Check out potential firms' and individual search consultants' track records. You don't want to work with a firm that blindly mails your resume to employers without your knowledge or consent or that doesn't keep you informed about the search they are performing on your behalf.

1. *Carefully select two or three firms (depending on the size of the job market you are interested in) to assist you.* If you are looking for a position in a large metropolitan area with a huge legal community, you may want to select a few firms. If the area is small, one firm may suffice.
2. *Interview the legal search firms you've selected, first over the telephone and possibly in person if you and they have the time.* The really good ones are probably too busy to spend a lot of time talking with you in per-

son. And some headhunters want to meet all of the attorneys they intend to work with.

3. *Ask the firm for professional references,* from both law firms they've worked with and from attorneys they've placed in firms. It raises a red flag in my mind if a legal search firm or individual consultant doesn't want to give you references. The best sources of information are often the satisfied clients.

4. *Call and check these references.* No one usually minds giving out this kind of information. Just tell the attorneys you speak with that you're considering using the firm, and ask them if they were satisfied with the results they received, if they would recommend the firm to someone else, and if they would use the firm again.

In addition, there are good legal-related directories in the marketplace that you may find useful in your selection process. The *American Lawyer* publishes an annual "Legal Recruiters Directory" as a supplement in its January issue. This is an invaluable source of information on legal search consultants. Placement offices and legal libraries often stock copies, or you can contact the *American Lawyer* directly at 212-973-2800 for more information.

WHY FIRMS USE LEGAL SEARCH CONSULTANTS

You may be asking yourself, "If law firms, especially the large ones, have experienced recruiting staffs, then why do they need to utilize the services of legal search firms?" There are many reasons:

1. *"Star" candidates will always be in demand.* Believe it or not, the old cliché "Good people are hard to find" is actually true, even in today's job market. Star candidates will always be in short supply. Law firms will probably always be willing to pay search firm fees for certain candidates, even if they aren't actively looking for them.

2. *Some "holes" left when someone leaves must be filled immediately— time is money in a law firm.* If a law firm loses a valuable associate in the middle of a big case and the clock is ticking, legal search firms are often the best resource to replace that individual immediately. Through their databases, they already know where the talent is to fill a needed position in another firm.

3. *Most law firms find it unethical to directly recruit attorneys from other law firms.* So they pay legal search firms to do it. In the current climate of

economic belt tightening, you might anticipate that law firms have discontinued this practice, for monetary reasons alone. Surprisingly, this is not the case. Almost every law firm I interviewed still uses legal search firms to fill lateral positions. Obviously, some firms utilize legal headhunters more than others, but there are still many legal search firms making huge salaries at the expense of law firms.

4. *Sometimes firms have too many positions to fill at once.* Some firms are still experiencing huge rates of growth. Even an experienced recruiting professional can't always do all the work. Often you'll find legal search consultants helping out in such cases.

5. *Some firms don't have recruiting staffs.* Small or medium-sized firms may not have the available manpower to fill lateral positions. So they call in the experts for help when they need it.

WHEN YOU SHOULD USE A LEGAL SEARCH CONSULTANT

There are circumstances in which it may make sense for you to utilize the services of a legal search firm from the very beginning:

1. *When your workload is so demanding that you have little available time to look for a new position.* If you find yourself so involved in work that you have zero time to prepare resumes, research employers, and make phone calls during working hours, then using a headhunter may make good sense. But don't use your heavy workload as an excuse to turn your job hunt over to a search firm if you really can manage to do it yourself.

2. *If you're relocating to an area you're not familiar with.* Relocating to a new, unfamiliar area can be difficult, especially if you are unable to spend time there researching the market and networking. A good headhunter knows the market and can help educate you on what you can expect in terms of job availability and salary levels. This may be your best resource under these circumstances.

3. *If you have no contacts in the market you want to enter.* As we discussed in Chapters 2 and 14, networking is an essential component of any job search. If you have absolutely zero contacts in a market, then using a headhunter may make sense.

4. *If your credentials are so incredible that any firm would be willing to hire you, regardless of whether they have to pay a headhunter's fee.* We'd all like to be in this predicament. Unfortunately, this rule applies

only to a very small percentage of the attorney population. For example, if you graduated from Yale, clerked for an appellate court judge and then the Supreme Court, and worked for two years in a major New York firm, then you can write your ticket to any destination.

WHEN NOT TO USE A LEGAL SEARCH CONSULTANT

While there are circumstances in which it makes good sense to utilize the services of a legal search consultant, there are situations in which it probably makes better sense for you to search for a new position on your own:

1. *If you're already familiar with the legal job market.* If you are planning to relocate to an area in which you already know the legal job market or if you're searching for another position in the market in which you are already working, then using a headhunter probably doesn't make good sense. As an example, one associate and her attorney husband decided to relocate to a city in the Southeast. She had a good friend who had previous contacts in the legal market there and was willing to make some phone calls on their behalf. They already had what it takes to start the ball rolling in their job search and had little need for the services of a legal search firm. I also believe that their search was easier, since neither had a headhunter fee attached to them. They were able to locate good legal positions very quickly on their own.

2. *If you've been out of law school for less than one year.* It makes law firms angry to see new associates who have just gone through the on-campus recruiting process using headhunters. Why would a firm pay a $25,000 fee for an almost entry-level candidate when they can hire someone six or nine months more junior for nothing?

3. *If you've recently completed a judicial clerkship and possess no full-time work experience in a law firm.* The same thought process applies here. Firms don't want to pay huge headhunter fees for entry-level or almost entry-level experience, especially when there are other candidates with similar credentials on the block without headhunter fees attached to them.

4. *If your new market is tough to crack and there is an abundance of candidates available.* Keep the forces of supply and demand in mind at all times. If the market is already saturated with candidates at your level and firms don't have to pay headhunter fees, they won't. You may not realize how tight your market is until you get in it, so do a little research early on to find out. Contact your law school placement office for assistance, or

make a few cold calls to headhunters in the area for information. Remember that firms won't pay headhunter fees if they don't have to.

5. *If you're making a career change of any kind.* Law firms are willing to pay headhunter fees only for candidates who exactly fill their needs. If you are an environmental litigator wanting to become a corporate finance attorney, it's extremely unlikely that a law firm will be interested in paying a headhunter fee to retrain you. If your goal is to take a different path in your law firm career, you should brush up on your networking skills.

6. *If there's a gap in your work history due to a sabbatical or a period of unemployment or if you're currently unemployed.* Law firms probably aren't willing to pay headhunter fees for candidates they perceive to be risks. While today it's not unusual to find candidates who have followed different paths—taken sabbaticals or time off to pursue other interests or to travel, for example—you may have a difficult time convincing a law firm that you are worth paying a fee for if you have done something out of the ordinary or if you have had a difficult time finding a job after being laid off or terminated. And if you're currently without a job, you will probably have a tough time as well. The adage "It's easier to get a job if you already have one" is true.

MARKETING YOURSELF IF TERMINATED OR LAID OFF

Law firms are tough places to work, and it's increasingly common in today's economic climate to find yourself laid off or even terminated for numerous reasons. While no one ever wants to be in this unfortunate position, it's not the end of the world, and many people manage to successfully pick up the pieces and move their legal careers forward despite these temporary setbacks.

But how do you present yourself positively to other potential employers once you've been fired or laid off? What do firms view as acceptable risks in lateral candidates in such situations, and what are the danger signs that make firms avoid certain lateral candidates, no matter what?

Get Letters of Recommendation Before You Leave

Regardless of your plight, always get several letters of recommendation from your most recent employer. Ask at least one partner to write a *formal* letter of recommendation on your behalf before you leave. If you can, get several recommendation letters from various attorneys you worked with in different practice areas. Letters of recommendation eliminate the need to check *every* reference, and multiple letters of recommendation may indicate that you are a valuable asset to many people and multiple practice areas, which may help broaden your appeal.

Be Consistent in Your Story Line

Before you begin your job search, establish a story line regarding your current situation, and stick with it. If you've been fired, construct, within the realm of reality, a valid reason for your predicament. And unless you've done something really awful to get fired, just tell the truth. If you had a personality conflict with your partner supervisor, if you just didn't fit in, or if you were doing work you really didn't like, just explain what happened.

If you did something that you're truly ashamed of or that will absolutely keep you from getting a job, that's another story. You don't always have to tell the entire world that you were fired, but you do have to establish a reason for being on the job market and *consistently* stick with it. Then make sure that whomever you use for references understands your reasons for changing jobs and gives the right story to potential employers. An inconsistent story line raises an immediate red flag. If a firm has even a slight suspicion that something fishy is going on, your chances for employment will be abolished immediately.

Never Act Desperate

Always put on a positive, happy face throughout the interview process, and *never* act desperate for a job. Your acting skills will come in handy again if you are, in fact, in a desperate situation. But too many job seekers don't realize that they come across as downcast. Act as though you have multiple choices, even if you don't, without being smug or arrogant.

You can accomplish this by indicating that you have several irons in the fire, are on second or even third interviews at more than one place. And *never* tell a firm that you will accept the position if it's offered to you. That makes you seem desperate, and it takes away any bargaining power that you have during the salary negotiation process. A despondent or desperate unemployed attorney stands out in a crowd and says "hands off." Trust me.

Keep an Office and Telephone Number
at Your Previous Firm

If your former law firm or employer will allow, maintain an office in the firm, with a phone number with voice mail or a secretary, for as long as possible. No matter what your current circumstances, this simply paints a better

picture to potential employers. Many law firms are generous toward departing attorneys, often granting them ample time to look for a new position.
And often, unless you are being fired for gross misconduct, firms will allow
you to use phone and secretarial services for ninety days or so. It's unlikely
that this benefit will remain open-ended.

If potential employers are able to call you at your office, they may think
you are still on the payroll there, even if you aren't. If your firm has, in fact,
given you a generous amount of time to locate a new position, this practice
can be very helpful. You'd be surprised at the number of attorneys who have
managed to find new positions soon after they'd been dismissed, without the
firm that just hired them knowing about the dismissal. While there is some
deception in this practice, I'm sure you'll agree that it's easier to get a job if
you already have one. Just make sure that you don't blatantly lie to a potential employer about your situation. If you tell the truth, you don't have to remember anything.

Utilize Outplacement Resources

If your firm offers outplacement assistance as a benefit, take full advantage
of it as long as possible. Outplacement firms are well versed in helping people overcome the negative connotations associated with being laid off or terminated. They are experts on teaching you how to turn negative situations
into positive ones, which, as you may discover, isn't an easy task. And you
may need counseling to keep your emotions intact during this stressful period. Many outplacement firms provide you with offices, telephone coverage,
resume preparation, job leads, and skill development workshops. You might
want to consider engaging an outplacement professional on your own if your
firm does not offer you this benefit.

17

THE LATERAL RESUME

"Got any good ideas for my resume?"

The lateral resume is an extremely important marketing tool. It's a key component of the recruiting process. Although a lateral resume differs in some respects from a student's resume, some basic ground rules remain. Law firms generally want more information from lateral attorney candidates and are less forgiving when errors occur. So it's critical that you do your homework and take the necessary time and effort to prepare a solid lateral resume.

HOW DIFFERENT FROM YOUR STUDENT RESUME?

There are some major and minor differences in lateral resumes that you should be aware of when putting yours together. I'll point some of these differences out for you to help you get started.

Work Experience Before Your Education

As a lateral attorney, you should always include your work experience first on your resume if you've been out of law school more than three years or so. Whether you've been working three years or not, once your work experience becomes more valuable to a firm than your raw academic credentials, it should be listed first, immediately after your name, address, and e-mail address.

For example, when you first graduated from college and started looking for a job, your educational background was at the top of your resume. At some point, your work experience became more important than your educational credentials. The same thought process applies to lawyers. As an experienced lateral candidate, you want your work experience to be the first paragraph on your resume. While your educational credentials are important, the first thing an employer is going to look for is your previous work experience.

One or Two Pages in Length

Unlike law students' resumes, a lateral resume can be longer than one page, especially if you have been working for more than four or five years. But don't make the mistake of filling your resume with information that is of little use to law firms just to make it fill several pages. Don't include every speech you have ever delivered, every division of the local bar association in which you've been a member, or every organization for which you have volunteered. Too much "filler" or "fluff" on a resume is just that, and it prevents the reader from finding the important information. And I've seen many excellent one-page resumes from lateral candidates with over ten years of work experience. Less is still more in my book.

More Targeted

The typical lateral resume should be more targeted than your student version. By this point in your career, you should have at least the beginnings of a specialty. When you prepare your resume each time for specific employers, you'll direct your resume to their areas of practice and needs. There are obviously some exceptions, such as attorneys practicing in small or rural areas, where general legal practices are still the norm. But more often than not, in today's legal market, as discussed in Chapter 15, firms want to see a certain level of specialization, and your resume should definitely make that distinction.

Prepare a Different Resume for Different Practice Areas

Because the lateral resume is more targeted, you should prepare a different resume for each practice area you are considering. If you happen to spend some of your time working in the securities and corporate finance area and the remainder of your work experience is in global custody work, you should focus your resume on one of these areas, depending on the needs and interests of your potential employer. But if you haven't done your homework, as discussed in Chapter 15, you really won't know who does what, and you may end up sending your global custody resume to a firm that doesn't practice in that area.

Include an Addendum if You Have a Significant Amount of Outside or Volunteer Experience

Instead of creating a verbose resume that may not get read, attach an addendum to your resume with additional information that may be of interest to an employer. For example, an addendum might include a list of your legal publications, speeches you have given, your community involvement, or your participation in bar activities. It may be critical to include this information if you think this experience is important to a potential firm. And some firms may never read your attachment, but at least your short, concise resume will get read.

WHAT LAW FIRMS LOOK FOR

In addition to your work experience, law firms look for many of the same basic credentials in their lateral candidates as they do for entry-level positions. As discussed in Chapter 15, if you had difficulty getting into a law firm as a student, you may find obstacles in your path as a lateral candidate. In addition to the basic academic criteria set by law firms, you need a certain level and type of work experience to get picked up as a lateral candidate. As a lateral candidate, your universe is much smaller. And because there are more pieces to the puzzle, finding a lateral position in a law firm is more challenging than getting in as a law student. But you can do it if you do your homework and target the firms that will want and need to hire you.

A Pattern to Your Experience

There should be a pattern to your work experience. Firms query candidates who have jumped all over the map. They prefer to hire individuals who have a logical progression to their work history. Making a career change into law or switching areas of practice midstream is considered acceptable. But if you have no rhyme or reason to your career path, law firms may worry, and your job search may be more difficult.

For example, a firm might question the motives, dedication, and work history of a candidate who, after law school graduation, worked in a law firm as a real estate attorney, then decided to go in-house and worked as a general corporate lawyer, then returned to a litigation-based firm, and now is interested in working in even another area in a firm. Your work history should demonstrate some stability, even in an environment that offers little of it. Firms take risks when they hire laterals, and you have to demonstrate that you are a risk worth taking before you can be seriously considered for employment. If your career has been all over the map, some of these obstacles can be overcome, but realize that your journey is going to be even more difficult.

Where You're Admitted to Practice

All law firms are interested in your ability to practice in certain jurisdictions and courts. This information should always be clearly visible on your lateral resume. Remember that some states require most attorneys to sit for the bar exam. Therefore, it can sometimes take almost a year to get admitted into practice in a jurisdiction. If time is of the essence, your lack of bar membership could hinder you from being a viable candidate for a firm. Do not hide this pertinent information by burying it somewhere in the text. Add a section at the bottom of your resume clearly indicating which bars you are a member of and in which courts you are allowed to practice.

RESUME RED FLAGS—AVOID THE DANGER SIGNS

There are danger signs—red flags—that experienced recruiting professionals look for and readily identify on lateral resumes. I'll give you a "heads up" on some of these so you can avoid some of the pitfalls that so many candidates fall into.

Someone Who Changes Jobs Every Two Years

There are individuals who simply move every two years or so. The reasons for changing jobs are often less important than the fact that the individual cannot stay in one place for very long. In the early years, these individuals are more difficult to spot, but after a while the pattern becomes clear. Firms often avoid these candidates like a plague. No one wants to hire someone who is going to move to the competition about the time they are finally trained and acclimated.

If you are guilty of this sin, realize that eventually it will catch up with you. Finding a new position will become more and more difficult as you add more employers to your work history. If you can, indicate on your resume or in your cover letter why you've changed jobs so often. This may help lessen the blow.

Someone Who's on the Market as They Approach Partnership Consideration

Firms usually query why someone who is up for partnership in the next year or two is on the job market. Automatically, whether fair or not, firms assume that these candidates know they are going to be passed over for partnership or perhaps have already been told they are inadequate partnership material. While this line of thinking may be unfair or inaccurate, firms often automatically jump to this conclusion.

If you truly believe you're going to be passed over, don't wait until the last minute. Think far enough ahead so that this red flag won't apply to you.

Someone Who's Changing Jobs After One Year on the Job

If you are changing jobs after only a short time (18 months or less), firms may sometimes automatically think you can't cut the mustard and either you are being asked to leave or you have seen the writing on the wall. While many attorneys change jobs early in their career for many reasons, you should make it very clear in your cover letter why you are on the auction block. An even bigger red flag is raised if an attorney clerked for the firm he or she is now wanting to leave.

A Senior Attorney with Little or No Portable Business

There's some truth to the law firm adage "Rainmakers never die." In today's economic climate, experienced attorneys are expected to possess some level of portable business. If you are a very senior associate (seven or more years of experience) or a partner and have nothing of tangible value to bring with you to another firm, law firms worry. In fact, you may have an extremely difficult time in the lateral job market without portable business after you reach this level. The economics of lateral moves will be discussed in Chapter 19. While the rules were changed several years ago and many attorneys were caught off guard and empty-handed, there has been adequate time to adjust to and play by the new rules. At a more senior level, you need to be able to bring business with you. Everyone can offer a firm experience after a while.

COVER LETTERS

The general rules discussed in Chapters 2 and 4 regarding law students' cover letters also apply to lateral candidates. There are some differences, however, of which you should take note:

1. *Your lateral cover letter should always explain why you are looking for a new position.* Firms always want to know why an experienced attorney is on the job market, and if that information is excluded, a worst-case scenario may be assumed. No news is not necessarily good news.

2. *Lateral cover letters should also be one page in length.* While a lengthy explanation of your circumstances may be necessary, no one willingly reads long cover letters. Remember that the purpose of a cover letter is to highlight points in your resume and to bring to light things that may not be readily apparent on your resume, such as why you are on the job market.

3. *You may also want to spend one paragraph briefly highlighting the more important aspects of your work experience.* The experience on your resume probably doesn't go into great detail because it would be too long, so a succinct cover letter is a great opportunity to add a little more information about what you have done, hopefully whetting the appetite of your reader. But make sure you don't disclose confidential or privileged information on your resume or cover letter. If you're an international tax attorney who worked on a precedent-setting case before the tax court, you might spend a few sentences describing your experience, going into a level of detail not found on your resume.

4. *Refrain from making negative comments in your cover letter about former employers. Never* make negative comments, especially in writing, about a former employer. Even if your former law firm sold your first-born child, find something nice to say about them, or say nothing at all. The line of thinking is that if you will make negative comments about one employer, then you'll say bad things about all of them. No one wants or needs to be bad-mouthed.

RESUME FOLLOW-UP

If you initially contacted a firm by mailing your unsolicited resume, then you should definitely follow up two or three weeks after mailing it. Follow the guidelines outlined for law students in Chapter 2. You're wasting your time mailing an unsolicited resume if you don't bother to follow up on it.

While this type of follow-up is crucial to your job search, I suspect that the majority of lateral candidates don't send their resumes out unsolicited through the mail. It's just too risky. Most lateral job contacts are made through networking or through legal search consultants. But you should follow up on your resume's progress in a firm, regardless of how it got there.

If you are using a legal search consultant, ask for a progress report every two weeks. This should include where your resume was sent, whether there is interest in you at these firms, and if you're already interviewing with several firms, a rough idea of the timetable. While it is sometimes difficult to pinpoint how long this process can take in firms, a reputable headhunter should be able to give you a general estimate or timetable.

Following up with the personal contacts you used to get into firms is tricky. They did you a favor, and you can't act like a pest, attempting to find out if they've made contacts on your behalf. Use your political savvy, and handle these situations with kid gloves—and every one will be different. But don't ever rock the boat. If your contacts don't do what they said they would for you, then there's really nothing you can do.

18

THE LATERAL RECRUITING PROCESS IN LAW FIRMS

"Based on my resume, what are my chances for partnership?"

The lateral recruiting process in law firms is more complex and takes more time than the law student recruiting process. Most lateral candidates don't realize how long finding a job often takes. Allow up to 90 days just for the interview process. If your goal is to change jobs in January, I'd start looking at least in June of the previous year. To be on the safe side, allow a good nine months for the process, from start to finish.

Many attorneys don't give themselves enough time simply because they don't know how the interview process works in law firms. Well, I'm going to tell you how it basically works so that when you plan your job search, it should be a little easier.

THE INTERVIEW PROCESS

Lateral candidates are often treated to the same luxuries as law students during the interview process. But often, the process is more complex, more planned and executed, and more in-depth than with law student candidates. Therefore, lateral interviews are sometimes more difficult to schedule and take more time.

Screening Candidates

Some firms thoroughly screen lateral candidates over the telephone prior to bringing them in for interviews, and others, if using a headhunter, expect the headhunter to prequalify the candidate. If your entrée into a firm was through your networking skills, anticipate that the firm will check you out at some point, perhaps even before bringing you in.

It's too risky to parade a stream of lateral candidates through a firm without first making sure they are viable candidates. Confidential conversations could be overheard, clients might see that the firm is interviewing lateral candidates from the competition and may not like it, and there's always the risk that the candidate's firm will discover that he or she is out interviewing. All of these situations can create negative feelings and ultimately hurt business.

Interviews

Lateral candidates, at all levels, usually interview with partners and with members of the practice group in which they would work if they joined the firm. Interviews are often thirty minutes in length, and a half-day interview schedule is common. You are often treated to lunch, cocktails, dinner, or sometimes more than one. It is common for a lateral candidate to return for a second round of interviews. In some cases, you may be asked to return for a third time if scheduling interviews with key attorneys in the firm proves difficult. Firms have their own requirements regarding which specific attorneys have to meet with lateral candidates before final hiring decisions are made.

Ask the firm you are interviewing with what its routine practices are for hiring laterals. And get them to tell you how long they anticipate the process to take from start to finish and whether they have just started interviewing candidates or if they're at the end of the process.

If a firm goes to the time and expense of bringing you in for several rounds of interviews, then you should assume that they have a genuine interest in you as a viable lateral candidate. Too much time and money are at stake (especially if interviewing only with partners) to waste your time and their attorneys' time. But do not get your hopes up even at this point in the game. You should always expect the unexpected, and never assume that you are going to get the job until you have an offer in hand. There are simply too many unexpected things that can happen to prevent you from getting the job.

KEYS TO A SUCCESSFUL INTERVIEW

Lateral candidates, like law students, are often ill prepared for the interview process. And many have not interviewed for years. As discussed in Chapters 4 and 6, when you interview, preparation is nine-tenths of the law. Take the time to do your homework before you get started. And remember that firms often expect more from experienced candidates and are less forgiving when mistakes are made. Below are some interview tips that you may find useful as a rusty lateral candidate:

1. *Bring a list of prepared questions with you that are suitable for experienced attorneys.* In Chapter 7, I showed you how to create good interview questions. You also should prepare thought-provoking questions as a lateral candidate. Your genuine interest in a firm is often displayed by the fact that you took the time to research them and therefore have prepared good questions. Firms think that you're not interested in them if you don't ask them questions, no matter how many years you've been practicing law.

2. *Leave arrogance at home.* Successful lateral attorneys, especially those with large amounts of portable business or with enviable connections, can come across as arrogant or cocky during the interview process. Leave that attitude at home or at least at your current law firm. If you have enough clout, you may be able to get away with it, but who really needs this kind of attitude?

3. *Have sound and solid reasons for changing jobs.* Make sure that whatever your reasons for changing jobs, you come across as convincing. And as we talked about in Chapter 17, be consistent. Getting mixed messages about your reasons for looking around is an immediate red flag. If you are ever perceived as a risk, the transaction will never take place.

4. *Treat the staff with respect at all times.* Even experienced attorneys, at any level, should treat the staff members with dignity and respect. No one wants to hire a jerk. This is a bigger red flag in some firms than in others.

5. *Ask to interview with associates as well as partners.* No matter how much experience you have, it's always a good idea to talk with attorneys at all levels in a firm. Their perspectives are often completely different, and it is in your best interest to get as complete a picture of the firm as possible. If your interview schedule does not include both partners and associates, ask to interview with both groups.

WHAT CAN GO WRONG DURING THE INTERVIEW PROCESS

There are numerous things that can go wrong during the lateral interview process that many candidates never count on. Many strong lateral candidates, who counted on offers that appeared to be coming down the track, have discovered to their dismay that a glitch or an unexpected development kept them from getting the offer they thought they had sewn up. The following tips can help you head off some of the more common "glitches":

1. *Have a general idea of your salary and partnership requirements.* There is an obvious place in the interview process for salary and partnership negotiations. But if your expectations on these issues are in a different galaxy than those of the firm, you're probably wasting your time as well as the firm's. Ask, in the very beginning, what the firm's typical salary ranges are and typically what kind of partnership credit they grant laterals.

2. *Determine early if any conflicts of interest exist.* If you have been involved in a case that may preclude you from working on cases at other firms, put these facts on the table at the beginning of the interview process. Sometimes Chinese walls can be built, shielding an attorney from working on certain matters, but clients often have to approve such arrangements. I've seen this break deals on several occasions, much to the chagrin of the attorneys involved. Don't let this happen to you.

3. *Never overestimate the amount of your portable business.* If ever in doubt about how much of your current business will walk with you to another firm, be conservative in your estimate. Lateral attorneys almost always overestimate how much of their business will "port" to another firm. Therefore, firms often discount your estimates. For example, if you claim to have $750,000 of portable business, a firm will assume that you have between $500,000 and $600,000. Tell a potential firm how much business you currently have, and then give them estimates on how much you *realistically* think will port. If you are completely off in your estimates, it can ultimately be a deal breaker. It's much better to claim to have $400,000 and end up with $500,000 than the other way around.

4. *Don't put all your eggs in one basket.* A change of plans is a regular occurrence in a law firm. Operational indecisiveness is common in law firms, especially when it comes to recruiting. **Never** assume that you have an offer until you receive it in writing. Therefore, have several irons in the fire in case the firm you thought was going to give you an offer doesn't come through.

HOW FIRMS WEIGH LATERAL CREDENTIALS

Weighing lateral credentials is not an exact science. Obviously, law firms rank and view laterals' credentials differently. Research performed by the National Association for Law Placement resulted in a "list" of credentials that are deemed important by law firms when recruiting lateral attorneys. While many of the items on this list are beyond your control to change, you can target firms, through your own due diligence, that may find your credentials noteworthy. NALP's list, which assumes that due diligence has been performed, includes the following factors:

- Prior employer(s) and history of mobility
- Expected fit with firm culture
- Quality of legal products
- Experience, expertise in specific practice area
- Law school attended
- Grade point average
- Honors, awards, recognitions
- Personality, drive, recognition
- Client following

Keep these factors in mind throughout the recruiting process, and attempt to ascertain which of these traits a particular firm deems most important. Indirectly ask firm members which traits they deem most important. If you are repeatedly told that all members of the firm attended prestigious law schools and you did not, you may be wasting your time attempting to go through the interview process. Find firms that will look upon your skill set and credentials in a positive light. You'll never find a 100 percent match, but learn not to waste your time seeking out firms with which you have little in common.

19

THE ECONOMICS OF LATERAL HIRING

"For tax-planning reasons, any chance of getting part of my compensation in cash?"

Law firm economics are no longer reserved only for managing partners and members of the management committee. It's imperative that all attorneys—associates as well as partners—understand how law firms operate from an economic viewpoint. Grasping the concept is necessary if you are planning to go through the lateral recruiting process. Many attorneys don't understand the economic implications inherent in hiring experienced legal talent. As firms become more operational oriented and look more and more to the "bottom line," you **must** begin to understand the economic implications of moving from one law firm to another.

SEARCHING FOR SALARY AND PARTNERSHIP INFORMATION

As we've already discussed, when you jump into the lateral job market, you should educate yourself on the markets in which you're interested in working, including researching the salary levels and the trends in granting partnership credit to lateral candidates. I've seen too many people who fail to educate themselves in the beginning on what the market will bear and later, after months of work, find out that their current situation is better than their other options in the marketplace. It doesn't make sense to waste time interviewing in a market in which you can't afford to work.

Legal Search Consultants

One relatively untapped source is legal search consultants. They know the legal market as well as anyone and often are open to giving you ballpark salary figures for specific levels and types of experience. Contact reputable headhunters in your potential market, and ask them to give you a reality check.

Local Chambers of Commerce

Contact the local chamber of commerce for salary and cost of living information on particular cities and regions. Keep in mind that salary levels are often relative to the cost of living in an area. For example, in the southeastern United States, legal salaries are much lower than in the Northeast. But the cost of living is equally as low. In fact, your standard of living may be higher in this region, even though the salary levels appear to be very low. There are also markets in which the salary levels are low in comparison with the cost of living. San Francisco is an ideal example of this phenomenon. The salaries in the Bay Area just do not measure up to the high cost of living there. Have a general idea of your cost of living threshold as you go into the interviewing process and know what your bottom line is.

Salary Surveys and Publications

There are numerous publications and surveys that you may find helpful as an overall resource but that may not be tailored to specific job markets. If you are looking at smaller markets, there may be less outside information available. Primary research on your particular market is often the best and most reliable, up-to-date source of information.

Altman Weil Pensa, Inc., a well-known legal consulting firm, publishes *Survey of Law Firm Economics* annually in May or June. This study includes information on fees, standard billing rates, earnings, and staffing ratios. Information is provided by practice area, size of law firm, geographic region, and metropolitan area size. The cost is $495. *The Small Firm Economic Survey* covers firms of two to five and six to twelve lawyers, and the cost is $225. Contact Joe Bello, Product Sales and Information Manager, at Altman Weil Pensa Publications, Inc., P.O. Box 625, Two Campus Boulevard, Newton Square, PA 19073; telephone 610-359-9900, extension 435, or fax 610-359-0467 for additional information.

For more than twenty years, David J. White & Associates has published *Attorney Salary Survey,* which comes out in September with information on attorney salaries in specific cities and by levels of experience. The survey covers thirty-three cities and contains information on salaries of associates with zero to eight years of experience, as well as information on partner salaries and corporate law departments. The cost is $195, and many law school placement offices subscribe to this publication.

David J. White & Associates also publishes two weekly reports that contain information on specific job openings. These reports are available in hard copy as well as online. *Position Report I* and *Position Report II* contain information on available law firm positions, government and in-house legal positions, and administrative positions in law firms. The cost for each publication is $43.50 for ten issues, and if you subscribe to both, you get a 25 percent discount on the second publication. For more information, contact David J. White & Associates, Inc., Village Center Building, 809 Ridge Road, Suite 206M, Wilmette, IL 60091; telephone 800-962-4947. The database number is 847-256-8836. In the future, look for this publication on the Internet and on the upcoming ABA Homepage.

The *National Law Journal* publishes an annual supplement, "What Lawyers Earn," in the May issue. This survey of salary information targets specific firms in specific cities, by associate class. Also included is salary information for judges, law professors, deans, public defenders, in-house counsel, and so on.

THE CONNECTION BETWEEN SALARY AND BILLING RATES

Law firms often tie associate salary levels to billing rates and partner compensation to the amount of business you bring in the door. When you negotiate your salary at a new firm, you should understand how your salary level will affect your billing rate, which ultimately will affect the amount of work you have, that is, your billable hours. Let me show you what I'm talking about.

First-year associates making $70,000 might have a billing rate two times their salary, or $140 per hour.[1] (Drop the last three zeros and multiply by

---

[1] Firms use different formulas to determine these rates. An average rate could easily be two times your salary, so if you're making $75,000, your rate might be $150 an hour. Some firms will use even larger multipliers. You should find out, during the interview process, what multiplier a firm uses.

two.) As associates progress up the ladder, gaining more experience, their billing rates and salaries also increase. As long as associates continue to develop their expertise, clients continue to pay their increasing rates. But if associates reach a point where they can no longer produce the quality of work expected at their experience level, and clients pick up on it, firms have to adjust rates or write off billable time. If this situation isn't remedied, these attorneys usually find themselves on the job market.

When you move from one firm to another, all things being relatively equal, you expect to continue this progression, moving up the ladder in terms of experience, billing rate, and salary level. But you have to be able to continue to do the work at your level of development, you have to be able to bill at a rate that justifies your salary, and within a relatively short period of time, you must make a profit for your law firm.

If you move around too much, continually throwing yourself backward in terms of experience, your salary level and billing rate will also lag behind. Changing areas of expertise or moving to markets where salary levels and billing rates are lower can alter the logical progression that many associates simply take for granted.

Problems That Can Occur

Lateral job moves can create a host of economic problems. Just make sure that you are aware of these implications before you decide to jump ship. The following are some of the scenarios in which this tends to happen:

- An associate moves from one firm to another but does not possess the same level of expertise and training as his peers in his law school class at the new firm. You always take a chance when you make a lateral move from one firm to another. You must be prepared to come up to speed very quickly.
- An associate is given salary and partnership credit for a clerkship, and she is expected to start out as a second- or third-year associate even though she is technically only a first-year associate. She must immediately perform out of her league and must come up the curve two or three times faster than her peers. Again, some are able to come up to speed quickly, while others are not.
- A fifth-year associate moves to another firm, getting the five years of partnership credit he wanted. He is up for partnership consideration within 18 months after joining the new firm. That time period is too short for the firm to properly evaluate him despite the promises he was made, so he is "put on hold." He would have been better off to have come in with less credit, so that he would not have been furloughed for partner-

ship consideration. Who knows how long he will remain stagnant, and in his mind that mark will always be on his record, despite his unique circumstances.

• An associate demands such a high salary that her billing rate is much higher than other associates in her class. Partners are hesitant to use her because her rate is so high, so the associate has little billable work, is unprofitable, and is ultimately terminated.

The moral of these stories: Understand the economic implications of making lateral moves in law firms at every level of development. These issues will only become more important as law firms look more and more to the bottom line. Educate yourself now so that you know how to make the right *long-term* decisions. If you make demands on your new firm, just make sure you can live up to the possible consequences. Shortsighted associates rarely ever make it to partner.

CHANGING JOBS AS A LATERAL PARTNER

As discussed in Chapter 15, it has becoming increasingly common in the current job market to jump from one law firm to another, even as a partner. Not too long ago, the practice of "cherry picking"—plucking partners with lucrative client bases away from their firms—was shunned and practiced only by "renegade" law firms. As clients continue to tighten their belts and shop the market for lower legal fees with multiple law firms, firms are more interested in adding partners to their letterhead who possess big books of portable business. Becoming a self-sufficient partner is more important than ever to your stability as a practicing attorney.

What It Takes to Move

Experienced legal search consultants indicate that a junior partner wanting to move to another firm in a large legal market should have a bare minimum of $350,000 of portable business to be seriously considered by another firm. A more experienced partner candidate (someone who has been a partner for more than just a few years) should possess at least $500,000 of portable business. And if you really want to be a player, you should have more than $500,000 of documented portable business, preferably in the range of $650,000 or more. Obviously, these figures will vary depending on the market you are in, so you need to be familiar with the requirements in your area before you start shopping the market.

As mentioned in Chapter 18, when you seriously consider moving from one firm to another, hoping to take your business with you, keep in mind the fact that firms often discount the amount of portable business you claim to have. So be conservative in your estimates because you can be assured that the firm considering you will be even more conservative in their estimation of your stated client base.

How Partners Move from One Firm to Another

Partners have just as difficult a time securing new employment as associates. As you move up the ladder, your options tend to either increase or decrease exponentially. There's little middle ground. But partners have their own sources to rely on when looking for a new position.

1. *It's who you know.* If you made it to partner, you obviously have multiple contacts in your legal market. At this point in your career, networking should be a relatively easy task. Very often, partners wanting to leave their current firm work behind the scenes using the contacts they've made over the years. They often have a general idea of which firms will be interested in them. And experienced attorneys often know from the start which firms they're interested in as well, especially if they only want to move across town.
2. *Legal search firms.* Sometimes partners wanting to make a move utilize the services of a legal search firm. Time is a factor, and many busy partners simply don't have the time to locate the firms that may be interested in them. Others want to make sure that they "shop" the market and exhaust all available opportunities. Confidentiality is another important factor. Headhunters can explore potential opportunities without divulging the name of the attorney. And some partners may not have the contacts in a market necessary to locate a new position. If moving to a new and unknown market, using a legal search firm may be a necessity.
3. *You're recruited.* Some partners find that they are being recruited by another law firm. You may not be on the market for a new position, but an offer may come along that you simply can't refuse. If a firm is attempting to develop a new area of expertise, often they'll go out and find a partner in another firm who has that expertise fully developed. A more junior partner who works in the shadow of a well-known attorney may find himself or herself faced with the opportunity of being number one in another law firm. Or another firm may lure you with a higher salary, more stock options, or the opportunity to open new offices abroad. Many attorneys are lured away from their current firms in this manner.

The Risks Involved

There is a great deal of secrecy involved in the partner job search, and it's often risky to place yourself on the auction block. You risk the chance that your current firm will find out you are on the market, and you risk your clients discovering that you are changing firms. Managing to leave your current firm on good terms, taking your clients with you, and remaining on good terms with your colleagues, all at once, is difficult at best. And often you do not know until the bitter end whether your clients are coming with you and which of your former partners truly are your friends.

How Long the Process Takes

The process of moving from one firm to another as a partner either tends to happen very quickly or takes much longer than the process as an associate. If your move isn't going to take place overnight, allow six to nine months for the process. While occasionally the switch happens very quickly, almost overnight, usually it takes much longer than you anticipate.

PART SIX

OTHER POSITIONS IN LAW FIRMS

The employer generally gets the employees he deserves.
—SIR WALTER BILBEY

20

PARALEGAL POSITIONS

"He says if we elect him to partnership before we terminate him,
it could simplify his job search."

L aw firms offer a variety of career options for nonlawyers as well as for
practicing attorneys. These positions utilize the talents of graduates from
trade schools, colleges, and business schools, as well as law schools. While
these jobs may not offer the upward mobility and variety often found in large
corporations, they satisfy the needs of many individuals interested in working in a comfortable, professional, and intellectually challenging environment. Moreover, the salaries and benefits for nonlegal positions are often
very competitive.

As a nonlawyer working in a professional position in law firms for almost ten years, I found that law firms offered me the ideal environment to
"do my own thing" without the rigidity of a large corporate structure. The
work was challenging, and the people were interesting, motivated, and service oriented. While I didn't have a career path with multiple options available to me as I might have had in a large corporation, in my mind the
trade-off was worth it. If I had to do it all over again, I would travel down the
same path.

One of the most well-known nonlegal positions in law firms is that of a
paralegal. Paralegals are often the unsung heros in law firms, laboring almost
always behind the scenes, doing much of the dirty work, taking little of the
credit. And paralegals usually make a fraction of the salary an attorney demands. But paralegal positions offer recent college graduates an immediate

entry into a law firm, often as a precursor to graduate or law school. Paralegal positions also provide trade and paralegal school graduates with a stable and challenging career path.

THE DEFINITION OF A PARALEGAL

You'll discover that different firms define the term *paralegal* differently. In some firms, paralegals are given huge amounts of responsibility, while in others, they are simply glorified clerks. The American Bar Association has come up with a generic description of a paralegal, which is a good place to begin our overview of the profession:

> Persons who, although not members of the legal profession, are qualified through education, training or work experience, are employed or retained by a lawyer, law office, governmental agency, or other entity in a capacity or function which involves the performance, under the direction and supervision of an attorney, of specifically-delegated substantive legal work, which work, for the most part, requires a sufficient knowledge of legal concepts, such that, absent that legal assistant, the attorney would perform the task.

So why would you choose to work as a paralegal when you could become an attorney with only three additional years of training? While many paralegals eventually attend law school, others find that the work is challenging and intellectually stimulating, without requiring the long hours, regular overtime, and dedication required of associates. Some paralegals intend to go to law school and ultimately decide that they are not willing or able to make the commitment to the job required of an associate. Others work in a firm for a few years and determine that law firm life does not suit them after all.

WHY FIRMS HIRE PARALEGALS

Firms hire paralegals to **assist** attorneys on cases, usually at a billing rate much lower than that of associates. Paralegals tend to perform much of the repetitious and less intellectual work for which clients will pay less than associate rates. The work can be challenging, but it can also become mundane and routine after a while. Paralegals also work in areas of the law that tend to be repetitive and administrative in nature, such as bankruptcy, estate planning, collections, and immigration, just to mention a few.

Paralegals are routinely hired to staff large cases, often litigation-related matters. When large amounts of manpower are needed to sort, review, organize, stamp, and index important documents, the paralegals are called in. It's not unusual in large litigation cases for a firm to engage twenty or more paralegals at a time, just for one case.

Despite what many aspiring paralegals and recent college graduates think, paralegals aren't typically hired to perform legal research. Some more experienced paralegals routinely research issues, but that's not the norm. When considering a career as a paralegal, remember that a hierarchy exists in law firms. Paralegals fall at the bottom of that pyramid, below the partners and associates. Whatever assignments the attorneys choose not to perform fall into the laps of the paralegal staff. Rest assured that the heady, intellectual work is usually devoured by the attorneys whenever possible, especially if clients are willing to pay higher rates to get the work done. And don't think that just because you attended Brown University that you will be allowed to perform legal research or that you know how to do it. Law firms don't work like that, and many Ivy-educated paralegals have been humbled after spending weeks indexing and filing documents.

PARALEGAL SCHOOLS AND TRAINING

Paralegal degrees, certificates, and courses are regularly offered by community colleges, technical schools, colleges, universities, and paralegal schools, which exclusively cater to the paralegal profession. Today some of the best colleges and universities offer paralegal degrees either as part of their regular curriculum or as an adjunct program.

Many colleges offer evening programs that can be completed in about a year and intensive summer day programs. Make sure that the program you choose is accredited by the American Bar Association. The curriculum varies among schools, but a typical paralegal program might include study in the following areas in addition to elective courses in specific areas of interest and outside internships:

Legal research and writing
Legal accounting
Litigation
Commercial and contractual relations
Law office administration
Administrative law or trusts and estates
Legal ethics
Constitutional law
Torts
Civil procedure

Additional study might be offered in the following areas:

Evidence
International law
Corporate law
Family law
Medical law
Environmental law
Bankruptcy
Health law
Evidence
Telecommunications law
Real property
Criminal law
Intellectual property
Government contracts

Admission requirements vary among schools. Community colleges may require only a high school diploma for admission. Some paralegal schools require a college degree for admission. At Georgetown University's Paralegal Program, for example, a minimum 2.5 college grade point average is required for admission. For students for whom English is a second language, a TOEFL score of 550 or above is required. And some schools require students to pass a basic accounting exam prior to enrollment.

PARALEGAL ASSOCIATIONS AND ORGANIZATIONS

There are numerous associations and organizations associated with the paralegal profession that provide educational programs, professional recognition, and certification for its members, as well as employment assistance. Contact the local bar association in your area or local colleges and universities for information on what is available in your area. The following are some national paralegal organizations:

American Association for Paralegal Education (AAFPE)
Post Office Box 40244
Overland Park, KS 66204
913-381-4458
Publishes the *Journal for Paralegal Education* annually. Contact for information on local chapters.

Legal Assistant Management Association
Post Office Box 40129
Overland Park, KS 66204
913-381-4458
Promotes the professional standing of legal assistant managers.

National Federation of Paralegal Associations (NFPA)
104 Wilmot Road, Suite 201
Deerfield, IL 60015-5195
312-940-8800
Publishes a quarterly newsletter, *National Paralegal Reporter*.

National Paralegal Association (NPA)
Post Office Box 406
Solebury, PA 18963
215-297-8333
Publishes a newsletter and offers publications through its paralegal
bookstore.

WHAT FIRMS LOOK FOR WHEN
HIRING PARALEGALS

What's the best avenue to take to become a paralegal? And how do law firms view paralegal training and experience? The answers to these questions vary tremendously among law firms. Some firms require a paralegal degree or certificate, while others require only a college degree. I recommend that you review the classified section of your local Sunday newspaper to get a feel for the paralegal market in your area. Contact local employment agencies that specialize in placing paralegals in law firms for information. Contact firms in your area, and ask them what requirements they typically like to see for their paralegal positions.

In large metropolitan areas such as New York, Washington, or Chicago, where there is always an abundant need for paralegal talent, often only a four-year college degree is needed to become a paralegal. In smaller, less transient markets, where overall less hiring takes place, you'll find that specific training may be needed. The larger markets usually require at least a 3.0 grade point average for paralegal positions, and often the more prestigious firms prefer to hire from the top undergraduate schools.

Firms always look for strong organizational skills, especially in litigation paralegal candidates. Attention to detail and the ability to narrowly focus on even the most mundane task are traits needed by all paralegals in any market.

You May Need a Specific Type of Experience

For some paralegal positions, firms look for specific types of experience, even at the entry level. For example, one firm that did a lot of medical malpractice work decided to hire an experienced nurse for a newly created litigation paralegal position. They found that it was too difficult for someone to work in this area without strong medical knowledge.

In firms with strong bankruptcy or immigration practices in which paralegals are given a lot of responsibility early on, previous related work experience is often mandatory. Often you'll find several paralegals working in these areas with different levels of experience. When a more senior paralegal leaves, the others move up the ladder, and someone is trained on the bottom rung by the more experienced paralegals. And some firms find that government agency experience is helpful for some paralegal positions in areas such as trade, antitrust, or telecommunications.

In the technical areas of law such as patent and intellectual property, very specific training and experience are needed. You may find that entry-level positions in these areas are difficult to locate, technical undergraduate degrees may be necessary, and engineering, biotech, or computer-related work experience is also useful. These positions also tend to pay better than the nontechnical paralegal positions.

OTHER AVENUES YOU CAN TAKE TO BECOME A PARALEGAL

There are many other avenues to becoming a paralegal besides specific schooling. You have a lot of options.

Promotion from Within

There are numerous accounts of employees who were promoted to paralegal positions after working as receptionists, secretaries, couriers, accounting clerks, and so on. Promotion from within is a common occurrence in law firms, and many individuals have worked their way into paralegal positions without the benefit of a college degree or paralegal certificate. Working your way into a paralegal position via this route takes time, sometimes several years, but if you set your sights on the right horizon and are willing to pay your dues long enough, you can achieve this goal.

How do you get promoted without having the required credentials or educational background in the current age of layoffs and downsizing? It is possible if you follow certain rules:

1. *Consistently give your position more than 100 percent effort no matter what you're asked to do.* Your steadfastness and dedication will help make you invaluable to your firm no matter what position you may be in.
2. *Make sure that your firm knows you're ambitious and want to do more, but do so without whining or complaining.* Be subtle in your approach, but be assertive (not aggressive) about your desire to improve your position.
3. *Make sure that your firm recognizes that you possess the skills necessary to be a paralegal, despite any educational deficiencies.*
4. *If you lack some skills, go out and get them on your own.* If you need strong research skills, even though you have no formal training, attempt to gain them in your current position, even if it means tackling the books on your own time.

One dedicated individual decided that he wanted to become a paralegal and ultimately attend law school, even though he entered his firm as a courier. He had no formal paralegal training. Throughout his tenure as a courier, he made it clear that he was ambitious and wanted to do and learn more. In his spare time, he managed to work for attorneys, completing paralegal-related assignments, while maintaining his position as a courier. His work as a courier never faltered, and the assignments he performed on the side were always top-notch. Even though the firm shied away from placing individuals from his department into paralegal positions, when the next paralegal position became available and the courier voiced his interest, the firm considered him. His track record spoke in volumes. Needless to say, he was promoted to the paralegal position, and he continues to perform like a star. His next goal is to go to law school, and I'm sure he'll eventually get there.

Work as a Temporary First

Another avenue often taken in today's legal job market is to work as a temporary paralegal in a law firm first. Many firms hire temporary paralegals on a regular basis, especially to staff large cases and to make sure a candidate works out before making the commitment to hire as a regular full-time employee. In many cities, there are personnel agencies that specialize only in placing paralegals in law firms. Review your Sunday newspaper, call local law firms, or thumb through the yellow pages to research this market in your area. This is an excellent vehicle to test the waters, both from your perspective and from the law firm's.

Working temporarily as a paralegal is becoming a popular entrée into a law firm, as firms are becoming more hesitant to add regular full-time employees to their pared-down staffs. Temporary firms report that they are receiving increasingly more requests for seasoned and entry-level paralegals from law firms. But the use of temporaries is not a one-sided affair. Many experienced paralegals are discovering that they can work as a temporary or contract paralegal, working only when it suits them, making a good hourly wage, but avoiding the career burnout ultimately experienced by many in the profession.

The Rotten Truth about Being a Paralegal

Paralegal positions in law firms offer many opportunities, but they can also be a dead-end track for ambitious professionals who want to progress down a primrose path. You should be aware of the limitations of the profession before your set your sights on becoming a professional paralegal.

YOU'LL EVENTUALLY "HIT THE WALL"

Many people who work in law firms fail to realize that the legal hierarchy is always black and white: You either have a law degree or you don't, and you're limited, no matter how smart or ambitious you are, by that fact. The law places limits on the tasks you or anyone else can perform in a law firm, based on the legal training you possess and whether you've passed a bar exam. That distinction *never* disappears. Your career path and your salary will *always* be limited by these factors. I'll use a marathon runner's term for this phenomenon—you'll eventually "hit the Wall."

Salary and Billing Rate Limitations

Ambitious paralegals who decide to remain in the profession for the long haul often become frustrated by the salary ceiling they ultimately encounter and by the limitations placed on them simply because they're not lawyers.

Billing rates are often tied to salary, and there is a divergence where paralegal rates become so high that they become associate rates. This is often the place where associates take over paralegal work. While there are some exceptions, it simply does not make sense for paralegals to bill at higher rates and make more money than associates when associates possess much more training and education. The same line of thought applies to the paralegal learning curve. The "topping out" effect troubles many ambitious paralegals, but the economics of the legal market make it unlikely to disappear. Understand where that learning curve peaks out in your area of practice, and make sure you can learn to live with it if you plan to remain in the paralegal profession long term.

PARALEGAL MANAGERS AND SUPERVISORS

Big firms with large paralegal staffs often hire managers to supervise this group of paraprofessionals. Paralegal managers or supervisors are not typically found in small firms and are often located in large litigation firms where large numbers of paralegals are routinely needed to staff complex, document-sensitive cases.

It's usually difficult to become a paralegal manager without strong legal administrative experience or previous paralegal work experience. Sometimes an experienced paralegal will be asked to take on this administrative position. Occasionally, personnel or recruiting directors will have this responsibility added to their roster of duties. The paralegal manager is usually responsible for hiring, supervising, and firing the paralegal staff in addition to overseeing the paralegals' work on specific cases. This position has frequently come under the ax in recent times as firms continue to downsize and eliminate layers of management, like the rest of corporate America. Therefore, the long-term future for these positions as well as their availability for budding administrators may become more uncertain in the future.

THE FUTURE FOR THE PARALEGAL PROFESSION

In recent years, the press has heralded the paralegal profession, hailing it as one of the up-and-coming professions of the 1990s and beyond. As clients continue to force law firms to operate more efficiently, the paralegal ranks should continue to grow faster than other areas of the legal profession. In fact, the paralegal profession, according to Carol Kleiman in *The 100 Best Jobs for the 1990s & Beyond*, is the fastest-growing semiprofessional job, expected to grow by 104 percent, adding 62,000 jobs by the year 2000. Much of the growth is fueled by the more efficient use of technology, which should free attorneys up to assign more responsibility to legal technicians, according to Kleiman. *The National Business Employment Weekly*'s *Jobs Rated Almanac* estimates that paralegal positions will increase 86 percent through the year 2005! There should be ample paralegal positions available for the coming decade, especially in the larger markets.

21

ADMINISTRATIVE
POSITIONS IN LAW FIRMS

"Before you get started, Mr. Finkley, may I compliment you on your tie? And that
smart-looking suit of yours? Wow, you obvious stay fit; squash? Tennis?"

There are a variety of administrative and supervisory positions available in
law firms, especially the large ones, which offer intellectually challenging work and a great working environment. As attorneys discover that their
talents lie in practicing law, not in running the operational aspects of their
law firms, they have delegated these tasks to experienced administrators.
And as clients continue to demand efficiency in the legal services performed
on their behalf, this trend should continue.

WHAT'S OUT THERE

Many people aren't aware of the variety of administrative positions that exist
in legal America. The following is a sampling of the jobs that are found in
many law firms:[1]

Administrator or office manager
Controller or accounting manager
Facilities or office services manager
Personnel or human resources director

[1] Note that these positions may be titled differently in various law firms.

Recruiting coordinator or director
Marketing director
MIS director or director of computer operations
Law librarians
Economist or trade analyst

While you may not find these positions in every law firm, many law firms now employ individuals in some of these positions. I'll talk about what is generally involved in each of these positions individually.

LEGAL ADMINISTRATORS

A legal administrator can be thought of as the office manager, the chief executive officer, or the chief financial officer of a law firm. A legal administrator runs the daily business operations of a firm under the guidelines established by the firm's partners or board of directors. The legal administrator often supervises the rest of the administrative staff and manages the budgetary process as well as the other routine administrative functions such as billing and collections, computer and information systems, human resources and benefits administration, facilities management, and so on. Administrators must wear many hats, are quite versatile, and are usually excellent managers.

The Job Requirements

The job requirements for a legal administrator vary, depending on the size of the firm. In very small firms, legal administrators are often former legal secretaries who have been with their firm for many years and were promoted into the position as the firm grew. These positions are similar to that of an office manager. At the other extreme, in very large firms, administrators are often certified public accountants with law degrees or M.B.A.s, or even both. In these firms, administrators are highly paid and may have a full staff working with them.

Where to Look for Positions

Finding an entry-level legal administrator position is very difficult. Usually you need five to ten years of solid administrative experience under your belt before you can even be considered for such a position. Getting into a large firm without an advanced degree and previous law firm experience is increasingly rare. Some firms go outside of the legal field to find talented administrators but look for administrative experience in a professional services firm, such as consulting, accounting, real estate, and so on, along with a strong educational background. If your goal is to eventually work in legal administration, it's useful to possess law firm experience, either as an attorney or as another member of the administrative staff before obtaining an advanced degree. Having a strong background in finance or accounting is also mandatory for these upper-level positions.

For further information on a career as a legal administrator, I suggest that you contact the Association of Legal Administrators, known as ALA. ALA was founded in 1971 "to provide continuing legal education for professionals who manage the business activities of law offices." ALA sponsors meetings and seminars and publishes a monthly magazine for its members. Many firms advertise for legal administrators through the national magazine or through the local chapters, many of which have monthly newsletters. Membership in ALA is also useful to legal personnel directors, MIS directors, and facilities managers. For more information, contact ALA at the following address:

Association of Legal Administrators (ALA)
175 East Hawthorn Parkway
Suite 325
Vernon Hills, IL 60061
708-816-1212
708-816-1213 (fax)

CONTROLLERS OR ACCOUNTING MANAGERS

There's almost always someone in a law firm who heads or supervises the firm's accounting department. All firms have accounting departments, but their structure and size vary tremendously, depending on the size of the firm. The individual who manages the accounting department might be a promoted legal secretary or an experienced accounting professional who is a licensed C.P.A. or has an M.B.A. Some firms delegate responsibilities of this position to the administrator or office manager. Like many administrative positions in law firms, many options exist for how this work is delegated.

The controller or head of the accounting department has a tremendous responsibility in any law firm. This individual oversees the revenue side— the inflow and outflow of funds, which enables a firm to keep its doors open. This is the area where the bills are paid and the money for legal services is collected. Payroll, if not outsourced, may also be handled in this department. It's safe to say that if the accounting department fails to do its job, everyone is very unhappy. The controller frequently works with the administrator in preparing budgets and working on projects that require an analysis of the firm's balance sheet.

Requirements for the Position

The person in this position often has previous legal experience. It is very difficult to come into this position without some prior knowledge of how law firm accounting departments work. In smaller firms, the controller often has worked his or her way up into the position, sometimes starting out as an accounting clerk. In the larger firms, where this department may be quite large, the director usually has a very strong accounting background, perhaps an advanced degree, and previous law firm experience. It is also becoming more important to possess above average computer skills, since the accounting departments are completely automated, even if the firm has a large computer staff.

Where to Locate These Positions

So how do you get into this area of a law firm? My first bit of advice is to plan to work your way into one of the top positions. You'll probably have to pay your dues for a little while and learn the ropes, especially if you have limited work experience. You will need an aptitude for accounting and numbers, which is often demonstrated by a college or technical school degree in accounting or previous work experience in accounting. Just don't expect to be able to walk into a director's position without some solid law firm accounting experience.

Firms frequently advertise for this position in the local newspapers or in local legal presses. If the position requires previous legal experience, you'll probably have better luck in the legal press or through a local chapter of the ALA. The salary ranges for law firm controller positions are usually good, and since all firms have accounting departments, finding these positions is not as difficult as for other administrative jobs.

FACILITIES OR OFFICE SERVICES MANAGERS

Facilities managers are responsible for maintaining the physical plant of a law firm—the buildings, grounds, individual offices, furniture, security, and equipment (other than computers and sometimes telephone systems)—as well as purchasing, maintaining, and overseeing supplies. This individual also oversees such functions as office moves, relocation, and remodeling and is called on to tackle space requirements associated with client needs such as rooms and equipment for document production, the storage of legal documents, leasing temporary space for cases, and so on. The facilities manager also has to jump through hoops, see in the dark, and land on speeding trains. I'm just kidding, but this is not an easy job. However, the duties of this position are sometimes delegated to other administrative positions in firms, often the legal administrator or office manager in small firms.

The Requirements for the Position

Like many administrative positions in law firms, individuals fall into facilities managers' positions through different paths. Because there is much heavy lifting and moving involved in this position, the individual found in this job is often, but not always, a man. A college degree is not mandatory, and many individuals found in this position have a military background. Strong organizational skills are required, as well as a general knowledge of building and mechanical systems. This is also an excellent job for someone who took early retirement but no longer wishes to stay at home.

The facilities manager often is responsible for supervising the "clerks' office" or mail room staff. This includes overseeing large copying projects, the delivery and receipt of all mail, and fax services. This aspect of the position demands strong supervisory skills and the ability to work with all types of people at all levels. Often, mail and fax rooms are staffed around the clock and on weekends. Facilities managers may find themselves working many nights and weekends, when duty calls. In other words, this isn't a typical nine-to-five administrative position.

How to Locate Positions

There's no secret recipe to locating a facilities manager position. If advertised, firms generally use the local legal press, the local ALA newsletter, or the Sunday newspaper. Promotion from within is not uncommon, especially if the facilities department is large. In many instances, this position is filled through word of mouth. Since the skills needed for this position are so varied, firms look for a certain "type" of person. You may even find it necessary to work in a large department and work your way up to the head position.

PERSONNEL OR HUMAN RESOURCES DIRECTORS

Law firm personnel directors are similar to personnel directors in other organizations in many respects. The personnel director typically hires people to fill staff positions, evaluates employees, disciplines and terminates individuals with unsatisfactory work performance, trains and orients new employees, administers the organization's benefits program, and completes and maintains the paperwork that accompanies these job responsibilities. A good personnel director, especially in the unforgiving environment of a law firm, requires strong counseling skills as well as a bedside manner. You must be able to counsel employees on how to perform to the best of their abilities, instruct them on how to get along with their peers, and counsel employees who may be laid off, fired, or promoted over their peers. Much of any good personnel director's day is spent behind closed doors, one-on-one with the staff members.

In a law firm, the personnel director has the added burden of keeping numerous partners happy, who often expect the same level of dedication from their staff as they do from their associates. This is a tough assignment in any environment.

What's Needed for the Position

You may think that working in personnel is an ideal job because of the large amount of human interaction involved. Strong communication skills are an absolute must for a position in personnel, but it takes much more than good listening skills. A good personnel director is usually not well liked, but is well respected by the staff. You must constantly discipline inadequate workers, while rewarding the superstars, keeping within the confines of the law. Knowing how to be assertive, not aggressive, and fair and impartial is paramount to the position. And possessing a thorough knowledge of employment law—well, that goes without saying. Even if your firm is lucky enough to have a labor law department, the personnel director must know the law well enough to function daily without that department looking over your shoulder.

There's no typical path to obtaining a personnel position in a law firm. Individuals arrive at this destination through many different avenues. Having law firm experience is important. If you look at newspaper advertisements for personnel directors in law firms, most require previous law firm experience. Many personnel directors were promoted through the ranks, starting out as secretaries or administrative assistants, working their way up by demonstrating loyalty, perseverance, and the drive and ambition to do more. Others started out as secretarial assistants to the director of personnel. Employment agency experience with an emphasis on legal hiring is another avenue you might consider. College degrees are now mandatory for these positions if coming in from the outside, but advanced degrees typically are not. An undergraduate degree in human resources is also beneficial and may demonstrate your interest in the field.

How to Find a Position

Legal personnel positions, if advertised, are usually found in local ALA newsletters, local legal newspapers, and the Sunday papers. But like so many jobs in today's market, many are never advertised and are filled through networking or word of mouth.

If you're interested in finding out what it takes to work in legal personnel in your own particular market, I would suggest that you contact several legal personnel directors for informational interviews. Ask them how they got to where they are, and ask them to advise you on a path to take in your market. Even the busiest personnel director does not mind taking time to talk with an ambitious aspiring personnel director. You may also want to inquire about the possibility of obtaining an unpaid internship to learn more about the field and to make contacts that may ultimately assist you in securing a position in the field.

RECRUITING COORDINATORS OR DIRECTORS

Many people believe that recruiting coordinators have one of the best jobs in legal America. In many respects, popular opinion is right. There are numerous perks inherent in this position. But what does a recruiting coordinator actually do, and how do you go about landing one of these prized positions?

What the Job Entails

First, let me explain what recruiting coordinators in law firms do to earn their keep. Again, these jobs vary from firm to firm, and some recruiting coordinators have much more responsibility than others. Some firms have large recruiting staffs, while others delegate this position to the legal administrator or personnel director. Nevertheless, I'll give you a general idea of the common responsibilities of an experienced recruiting coordinator.

The primary responsibility of a recruiting coordinator is to manage the attorney hiring function in a law firm. This involves receiving, reviewing, tracking, and answering inquiries from attorneys and law students for attorney employment and running the fall interview program. There is a cyclical nature to the legal recruiting process in law schools so that all on-campus interviewing takes place in the fall. Attorneys are sent on-campus to interview students, some of whom are then invited back to the firms for interviews. This process was discussed in detail in Parts II and III. Recruiting coordinators run this process, and in some cases, they do the on-campus interviewing. This process starts around Labor Day and runs until Christmas. During those months, most recruiting coordinators can only be reached at work.

Recruiting coordinators are also responsible for running the law firm's summer program for law students. This summer internship program is the primary vehicle firms use for hiring associates. Recruiting coordinators set up and run these program. Some firms have very elaborate summer programs, with twenty-five to fifty students. Other firms hire only a few students for the summer. The recruiting coordinator, in essence, plays "den mother" or "cruise director" during the summer months, supervising this group of students. The students are put to work and are closely evaluated, but they are also elaborately entertained at some firms. Again, recruiting coordinators, or members of their staff, plan and supervise the social events that are an integral part of this program.

So what do recruiting coordinators do during the rest of the year? Some recruiting coordinators have other responsibilities tacked on to their job descriptions. Some hire and supervise paralegals, some hire staff members, some have marketing responsibilities, some are involved in associate training and evaluations, and so on. The possibilities are endless, and you'll find all sorts of combinations in firms.

While it is true that the work of recruiting coordinators is quite cyclical—they are very busy from May to December—their primary responsibilities also occur all through the year. Legal hiring takes place twelve months a year. Lateral and first-year hiring can take place at any time. And planning a large summer program can take months, even if you have a staff in place to assist you.

How to Land a Position

So how does one obtain one of these unique positions? And where does the best market exist for these jobs? There is no magic route to becoming a recruiting coordinator. People with all types of backgrounds have landed these positions, but there are some tips you can use to help your search:

1. *Go to the large metropolitan areas.* Recruiting jobs are more abundant in the big cities, where there are more large law firms—New York, Washington, Chicago, Los Angeles, San Francisco, and so on. The

larger the firm, usually the larger the recruiting staff. Many small firms don't have recruiting departments, delegating these functions, if they are needed, to other members of the administrative staff. Your best bet is to target firms with more than thirty attorneys for these jobs.

I'd recommend relocating to a large city if your primary goal is to become a recruiting coordinator in a law firm. In smaller metropolitan areas, only a few jobs may exist. For example, in North Carolina, where I once worked as a recruiting coordinator, there were only five or six recruiting coordinator positions in the entire state! Even today, only a handful of these jobs exist in this market, and they don't turn over often.

2. *Work as a recruiting assistant first.* One route, which many people take, is to work as an assistant to a recruiting coordinator or as a secretary to the recruiting staff. Promotion from within is common in these jobs, if you first possess some basic credentials, such as a college degree. Pay your dues for a few years, and then wait to get promoted.

3. *Work in an employment agency.* Some have entered the recruiting field after working in a legal employment agency first.

4. *Work in a law school placement office.* Some firms will consider you if you have experience in a law school placement office, too. Law school placement personnel usually know the recruiting coordinators in law firms. This is an excellent springboard into law firm recruiting.

The governing organization of the legal recruiting industry is the National Association for Law Placement. Based in Washington, D.C., NALP offers its members, primarily recruiting coordinators and law school placement directors, educational opportunities, excellent publications, and a job listing service in its monthly newsletter. NALP's staff is extremely helpful. For more information, contact NALP at the following address:

National Association for Law Placement (NALP)
1666 Connecticut Avenue, NW
Suite 325
Washington, DC 20009-1039
202-667-1666
202-265-6735 (fax)

MARKETING DIRECTORS

Law firm marketing directors are a relatively new phenomenon in legal America. These individuals have appeared on the legal scene only during the past ten years or so. As law firms have become more marketing oriented, attorneys have realized that they know little about selling their services to clients and have thus delegated the marketing function to nonlegal marketing and public relations experts.

Like many legal administrative positions, the best opportunities for legal marketing experts exist where the big firms are located—the large metropolitan areas. Most large law firms in any part of the country now have a marketing director, but these positions open up infrequently, so your best bet is to go where the most jobs exist. Consider the Washington, D.C., New York, San Francisco, Chicago, Atlanta, and Los Angeles markets, for example.

How to Find a Position

Like recruiting coordinators' positions, it's tough to obtain a marketing director's job without marketing or legal experience. Ideally, you should have both. But since marketing positions in law firms are relatively new, there aren't too many people out there with a lot of experience. That's great news for those with the experience, and it's good news for those with marketing, but not legal experience. Firms almost have to consider individuals with nonlegal marketing experience because those with both are somewhat rare and expensive. So if you have solid legal marketing experience with a reputable firm, you can almost write your own ticket.

But if you don't have legal marketing experience and you are unfamiliar with legal markets, what's the best avenue to take to find one of these positions? Many who are in law firms got there in one of two ways—either they worked their way into the job from another position within the firm, or they did work for a firm first as an outside consultant. Those who worked their way into marketing positions were once working in administrative areas such as recruiting or personnel. Sometimes you find assistants who worked their way into the head position.

What happens more frequently, however, is that the individual did freelance work for a law firm and ended up being hired by the firm for the marketing position. Plenty of legal marketing directors once worked as outside public relations consultants, writers, advertising administrators, and so on. They had experience on the outside that could be transferred to law firms on the inside, but they had to learn how law firms operate, much to their dismay.

You Need Marketing Experience

The fact is, though, that you really need marketing experience, preferably in a professional services environment, to be a viable candidate for a legal marketing director's position. A college degree is absolutely necessary, and firms like to see master's degrees, preferably an M.B.A. I suggest that if you want to work in the field and have little experience, contact experienced marketing directors in law firms for advice. They can help guide you in your particular market.

The legal marketing field today reminds me of the legal recruiting industry about ten years ago. Back then there were few people around with real experience. People fell into the field and developed expertise. Now, it takes limited legal experience to get into the field. It takes some marketing experience to get into legal marketing, but not like it will be in a few more years.

As you might expect, legal marketing directors are a networked group, and their connections are used to help one another. The National Law Firm Marketing Association is an excellent resource for information on this field. There are many local chapters as well. The national organization can tell you where the local chapters are. You don't have to be a law firm member to join. Contact them for more information:

National Law Firm Marketing Association
60 Revere Drive, Suite 500
Northbrook, IL 60062
847-480-9641

MIS DIRECTORS AND RELATED TECHNICAL STAFF

Like many administrative and technical positions in law firms, MIS director positions and the support positions that often go along with them vary tremendously among firms. Usually, the larger the firm, the larger its technical staff. And an MIS position in a small firm is often very different from one in a large firm. Many people familiar with law firms would agree with me when I say that law firms have typically lagged behind corporate America in terms of their efficient and cutting-edge use of technology. But as the world becomes more automated, the use of technology and the technical staff necessary to keep systems up and running in law firms should become even more important than they are today.

In all but the smallest firms, you'll usually find an MIS director or someone who is in charge of the firm's computer system. These positions are now evolving into a highly skilled, technical, extremely important function in a law firm. But what you often find, a remnant from the past in many cases, is someone who has little formal technical training who was promoted into the systems position. As technology advances, these individuals, no matter how dedicated they are, often lack the skills necessary to keep up with the changes in the field.

In the large law firms, you often find large technical staffs. For example, one well-known East Coast firm has a nineteen-person computer staff. While this group of people services branch offices, to a degree, from the home office, its importance to the daily functioning of the firm cannot be overemphasized. As an example, this particular staff consists of the following personnel:

Three to four trainers
Training manager
Network manager
Three to four assistants to the network manager
Hardware manager
Manager of the UNIX-based accounting system
Help desk personnel—four to five people
MIS manager and assistant

In each branch office of this firm, there is an MIS director and several assistants, depending on the size of the office.

What the Job Entails

What does an MIS director and the related staff do in a law firm? In a firm like the large East Coast firm just mentioned, the director is largely an administrator. I hate to use the term "paper pusher," but often in larger environments, the MIS director prioritizes and delegates to others on the staff. The director makes the big decisions about what needs to be done when and by whom. In smaller firms in which the staffs are smaller, the MIS director will delegate if and whenever possible, but he or she will actually do some of the technical work or hire outside consultants to come in.

A normal day (if there is such a thing in a law firm) might consist of duties such as fielding calls from users, routine network maintenance, performing or supervising cabling work when computers are moved or added, telephone maintenance, training new users, training current users on new software, working with attorneys in supplying technical support for specific cases, preparing budgets, monitoring expenses, working with outside consultants to assist with work that can't be done in-house, and so on. It's a busy, never-ending job.

What Firms Look For

It's apparent that there are numerous opportunities in the larger firms for individuals with an interest in computer technology. This is also an area in which previous legal experience is not always necessary. In fact, many people have told me that they would prefer to hire people for these positions who have never worked in a law firm in order to gain real-world technical experience. Firms sometimes hire away from the consultants they bring in to do the work that the staff can't handle!

How to Find a Position

Where should you look to find these positions? Read the newspapers and local legal press. Contact law firms directly once you narrow your focus on a particular geographic area. Like many computer-related positions, there is more demand than supply at the present time, so if your skills are good, you shouldn't have trouble finding a position. But unlike some computer-related positions where you may be able to lock yourself away in a room for days on end, in a law firm you will probably have to interact more with people at all levels. The attorneys want to be involved in the decisions that affect their firm, and this often includes how the computer system works. Your problem-solving skills should be excellent, as well as your ability to work well under pressure with all types of people.

LAW LIBRARIANS

Many law firms have librarians on their staff. This resource is often a necessity in law firms, since attorneys and other staff personnel perform research on a daily basis. Getting the information they need quickly is vital to the operation of a law firm. The size of the library staff varies from firm to firm. Obviously, large firms will have bigger staffs than their smaller counterparts. The head librarian usually supervises any additional library personnel.

What the Job Entails

The librarian often acts as a go-between—between the attorneys and whomever has the written information they need. The attorney tells the librarian what he or she wants, and the librarian knows where to find it. A librarian also instructs the attorneys on where to search for their own information. After a while, a good law librarian learns to anticipate the needs of the attorneys and has the information they routinely want even before they ask for it. An experienced librarian who is familiar with the law firm's practice areas knows what information is routinely useful to the attorneys. Since attorneys are in the business of selling their time, an experienced librarian is worth his or her weight in gold.

Other duties that come under a law librarian's domain include budgeting, routing materials to the proper attorneys and staff members, shelving books, keeping the library clean and organized, training, and performing computer research for attorneys and staff members. An assistant may also perform some of these functions.

The Skills Needed for the Job

Many, but not all, law librarians possess master's degrees in library science. In the larger markets where there is more competition for jobs, you may find that you have to possess an advanced degree. In some jobs, such as legal academia, law librarians may even have law degrees. You definitely need an undergraduate degree, even for an assistant's position. But others get in the field by working as assistants and eventually work their way into the head position.

It's becoming increasingly important to have strong technical skills for this position. Familiarity with Lotus Notes, Dialogue, Dunn & Bradstreet, the Internet, the World Wide Web, and other databases is becoming more the norm than the exception.

Also keep in mind that a librarian is in a helping profession. Nurturing and problem-solving skills are absolutely necessary. You also must like working with people.

If you're considering getting into this field, talk first to some experienced law librarians for advice. They may guide you in your job search. If you possess a master's degree in library science, your school placement office is an excellent place to begin your job search. Many firms post their jobs with area schools. Also check out legal trade publications in your market. If a firm needs an experienced librarian, this is where they may advertise. Also look in your Sunday newspaper, especially if you are looking for an entry-level or assistant's position. Another excellent resource is the American Association of Law Librarians. Contact them at the following address:

American Association of Law Librarians
53 West Jackson Boulevard
Suite 940
Chicago, IL 60604
312-939-4764

The Future for Law Librarians

The law librarian as we know the position today is also likely to be altered as technology continues to change the way we receive information. In the near future, look for books to be put online instead of being housed in a firm's library. Information, which today is received on a weekly, monthly, or annual basis, will appear every morning on our computer screens. Since we can't look into our crystal balls to determine how radically technology will change the law library as we now know it, we can anticipate that technology will make a noticeable impact. Keep these future changes in mind as you look at this profession in particular.

ECONOMISTS AND TRADE ANALYSTS

Some law firms hire economists or trade analysts to assist attorneys with dumping and countervailing duty cases, common areas of an international trade practice. It's more likely that you'll find these positions in areas of the country such as New York, Washington, D.C., San Francisco, or Los Angeles, where import, export, and regulatory trade-related activity routinely takes place. Many individuals, especially entry-level candidates, lack a clear understanding of what economists and trade analysts do in law firms. Let me start by discussing the role of a trade analyst in a law firm.

What a Trade Analyst Does

In some law firms, a trade analyst performs the same functions as an international trade paralegal, while in other firms, a trade analyst may have years of experience and does much more substantive work. Generally, trade analysts keep abreast of the regulatory changes taking place within government agencies such as the Commerce Department, the International Trade Commission, the U.S. Trade Representative's Office, the White House, and on Capitol Hill so that they are then able to keep the attorneys abreast of policy developments.

Additionally, a trade analyst may monitor events in the Court of International Trade in New York or at the Court of Appeals for the Federal Circuit in Washington, D.C. International trade cases are first appealed to the Court of International Trade. Further appeals take place in the Court of Appeals for the Federal Circuit, better known as the CAFC.

Other duties that are routinely performed by trade analysts include incorporating trade-related data into briefs for the attorneys, simple preparation of data, and general research. Trade analysts need to be well connected on Capitol Hill as well as plugged into the various trade-related government agencies. The connections needed to obtain this information are crucial and cannot be overemphasized. Many law firms supply trade-related information to their clients before it hits the newspapers and trade journals. Having this inside edge is critical.

What an Economist Does

Economists are often brought in to complete the economic analysis inherent in dumping and countervailing duty cases. Dumping takes place when a U.S. industry alleges that a foreign company is dumping its products in the United States below what it costs to make it in their home country. Companies "dump" to establish a foothold in a new market or to sell more products in a market. Countervailing duty is when a country subsidizes an industry. For example, the United States subsidizes the American steel industry.

In dumping and countervailing duty cases, there is an enormous amount of economic analysis to be done. While some of this work is performed by trade analysts, the complex work is often handled by economists, many of whom possess master's degrees or doctorates. Since the Commerce Department uses SAS programming for these cases, those working on the law firm side need to be thoroughly familiar with this computer program.

How to Land a Position

Firms hire trade analysts and economists in a variety of ways:

1. *Entry-level positions.* Entry-level analyst positions or international trade paralegal positions are frequently filled by recent college graduates who possess an interest in trade. The competition is fierce for these positions, and in the larger markets, often only Ivy League graduates are hired.

2. *Experienced analyst positions.* Trade analysts usually possess more experience, often from a government agency. An accounting or economic background is always helpful due to the technical and precise nature of the work. Possessing a purely political science or foreign service background can take you only so far in this field. The government agency connections, however, are critical. There are individuals who have managed to create the relationships needed for these positions from scratch, but that's tough to do, and it may take several years to solidify the connections you need.

3. *Economist positions.* There are few substitutions for the background needed to become an economist, even in a law firm. The educational background has to be there—at minimum a master's degree in economics and preferably a Ph.D. Strong technical skills are also necessary, and Capitol Hill or agency experience is extremely helpful, although not mandatory. Many who possess these skills leave the government only to become highly paid consultants to law firms. They're the smart ones.

Where to Look for Openings

There are numerous trade journals that firms advertise in. Consider looking at *Inside U.S. Trade, International Trade Reporter, Congressional Monitor,* or *Daily Report for Executives.* Your Sunday newspaper is another source, and sometimes you'll find these positions advertised in local legal newspapers. The trade world is a close-knit group in which everyone seems to know everyone else, so you may find that word of mouth is your best source for finding employment. I would highly recommend talking to experienced trade analysts or economists for their insight into their particular market before you begin your job search.

22

LEGAL SECRETARIES AND OTHER CLERICAL POSITIONS

"I understand your bent for litigation work, Mr. Furman, but we've not had a court
stenographer sit in on an interview before."

Despite what many attorneys think, law firms probably couldn't function without legal secretaries. They're the ones who really know how to get things done in a law firm. There are even some experienced legal secretaries who probably know enough about the practice of law to pass the bar exam. And in my opinion, even the advances of computer technology won't eliminate the need for an experienced legal secretary or administrative assistant.

You may be asking yourself about now, "What's so great about legal secretaries, and what do they know that makes them so indispensable?" They know plenty. It takes more than just good secretarial and computer skills to become a legal or administrative secretary. (I'll use the term "legal" secretary, but you can substitute "administrative" if you prefer.) I'm probably being a bit overzealous, but legal secretaries seldom get the credit and recognition they deserve, and they are extremely hard to find, even in today's tight job market.

WHAT LEGAL SECRETARIES DO

Good legal secretaries become the right arm of their attorney boss. They eventually learn enough about the practice to anticipate the attorney's needs even before a request is made. Again, I'm not trying to patronize the profession, but good legal secretaries run the attorney's office in such a way that when the attorney is away, he or she doesn't have to worry about something falling through the cracks, because it won't. Legal secretaries are able to manage the administrative functions of the legal practice and recognize the types of emergencies for which the boss should be contacted.

The Many Hats of the Legal Secretary

Legal secretaries wear many hats. They type correspondence. They keep files up to date and organized. They answer the phone and send faxes. They greet clients. They keep track of attorneys' time and billing records and send bills to clients. Some even make collection calls and repair the computer system. In smaller offices, legal secretaries may act as the office manager, purchasing agent, or personnel director. In essence, legal secretaries do whatever it takes to keep the law office running smoothly—or at least the offices of the attorneys they work for.

If you do a little research, you'll quickly discover that legal secretaries are highly paid in any job market. They earn more than associates in some cases and are possibly the highest-paid type of secretary or executive assistant in the marketplace. I think that only administrative assistants to the very top executives are paid more. Good legal secretaries are worth their weight in gold, literally. Keep in mind, however, that the operative word is *good*.

What It Takes to Become a Good Legal Secretary

So how do you become a legal secretary, or more important, what does it really take to become a good one? It is clear that not every secretary or administrative assistant in the marketplace has what it takes to join this elite group. Picture this:

1. *Legal secretaries must have good skills*—typing, taking dictation (yes, some people still use it), excellent proofreading and editing skills, the ability to learn new software packages easily, basic accounting skills, and exceptional organizational skills with a strong attention to detail.
2. *Legal secretaries possess a special level of dedication and steadfastness.* Not everyone has this. And I'm not talking exclusively about working long hours, even though that's sometimes necessary. You have to be

willing to go that extra mile—to put the practice of law first, from time to time. When you know it's imperative to be there, you are there.

3. *Legal Secretaries have to be able to **never** let the ball drop*, which requires dedication, conviction, and the ability to focus 120 percent on a job until it's completed. Few people today possess those skills.

Other Requirements

What type of training is needed for these positions? The skills must be there, so whatever type of education is necessary for you to gain them is acceptable. Some legal secretaries have college degrees, while others barely made it through high school. Technical or secretarial school training is useful, but not mandatory. You may find it difficult to enter a law firm with no secretarial or administrative experience, but again, I've seen some really good secretaries with the right attitude and a strong foundation from which to work in firms become excellent, highly paid members of a firm with little previous experience.

You need good basic skills, but the rest is up to you. They sky can be the limit in a sense. I believe the following poem sums it up nicely. This poem has been going around law firms for years, and I'm not sure who wrote it, other than I'm sure it was written by a legal secretary. Or perhaps her boss wrote it.

The Legal Hierarchy—Who's on Top

The Circuit Court Judge

Leaps tall buildings in a single bound,
Is more powerful than a locomotive,
Is faster than a speeding bullet,
Walks on water,
Gives policy to God.

The County Court Judge

Leaps short buildings in a single bound,
Is more powerful than a switch engine,
Is just as fast as a speeding bullet,
Walks on water if sea is calm,
Talks to God.

The Senior Law Partner

Leaps short buildings with a running start and favorable winds,
Is almost as powerful as a switch engine,
Is faster than a speeding BB,

Walks on water in an indoor swimming pool,
Talks with God if special request is approved.

The Junior Law Partner

Barely clears a Quonset hut,
Likes tug-of-war with a locomotive,
Can fire a speeding bullet,
Swims well,
Is occasionally addressed by God.

The Sole Practitioner

Owns tall buildings but is in default,
Tears up tracks and derails speeding trains,
Keeps pistol in his desk,
Passes water,
Uses God as an expletive.

The Associate

Makes high marks on walls when trying to leap tall buildings,
Is run over by locomotives,
Can sometimes handle a gun without inflicting self-injury,
Talks with animals.

The Law Clerk

Runs into buildings,
Recognizes locomotives two out of three times,
Is not issued ammunition,
Can stay afloat with a life jacket,
Talks to walls.

The Law Student

Falls over doorsteps when trying to enter buildings,
Says, "Look at the choo-choo!"
Wets himself with a water pistol,
Plays in mud puddles,
Mumbles to himself.

The Legal Secretary

Lifts tall buildings and walks under them,
Kicks locomotives off the tracks,
Catches speeding bullets in her teeth and eats them,
Freezes water with a single glance,
She is God.

How to Find a Position

You have many options in terms of looking for a legal secretarial position. If you already have legal experience, finding a new position is a piece of cake. If your experience is limited, your job search will be a little bit more difficult, but not impossible. I'll point you in the right direction.

1. *Check out the Sunday newspaper.* There are always legal secretarial positions in the paper. Since these positions are often difficult to fill due to the law of supply (not enough of it) and demand (lots of that), many firms keep ads running all of the time.
2. *Use a personnel agency.* Law firms use agencies frequently to fill legal secretarial positions. Don't be afraid to contact them as well. In the larger markets, there are agencies that specialize in legal secretaries. (That tells you a little about the market.)
3. *If you attended a secretarial or trade school, contact the placement office.* Many have job banks and newsletters with job openings for their graduates.
4. *Contact law firms directly.* This may be a tough assignment if you're in an area in which there are lots of firms and you aren't familiar with them. Some firms are better to work for than others. But if you know the firms you're interested in, call the personnel director, and then fax or mail your resume. Make sure, however, that you follow up a week or two later.
5. *If your experience is limited, you may have to rely on the "N word."* Networking may be necessary. Contact any friends you may have who work in law firms. If they put in a good word for you, then a firm may be willing to take a chance on an unknown entity. And many firms give referral bonuses to staff members who help them fill positions.

It should be readily apparent that you have many options when it comes to locating a position as a legal secretary. It's really all up to you.

OTHER NONLEGAL POSITIONS IN LAW FIRMS

Up to this point I've only talked about the administrative and managerial nonlegal positions in law firms. There are several other types of positions that provide excellent jobs for many people, perhaps with lesser technical skills or ambitions. Nevertheless, these positions are an integral part of any law firm, providing excellent sources of work and income for many, and they're worth considering if they match your skill set and career track.

I talked about legal secretaries earlier in this chapter. While the legal secretary may be the majordomo of law firms, there are other secretarial positions in firms that don't require that level of dedication or experience. Word processors, floater secretaries, entry-level secretaries, receptionists, and general clerks are all positions that fall into this category. And they are certainly worth exploring as an employment option.

Word Processors

Many law firms have word processing staffs who do nothing but straight typing or word processing on a computer. Some firms have word processing centers that operate two or more shifts, six or seven days a week! These are great jobs for individuals who want and need predictable schedules and for those who want to know exactly what they'll be doing at work every day. A premium is usually paid for second and third shift work. Word processors are typically well paid for their work, too.

Floater Secretaries

Floater secretaries are hired to work wherever extra help may be needed in a law firm. Often firms use floaters as an alternative to calling a temporary employment agency. Floaters are familiar with the firm and know how things operate, which makes integration into unfamiliar areas easier than when using a temporary secretary. A floater might fill in for someone who is ill or on maternity leave, or a floater might work in an area where there is an unusually heavy workload. Sometimes floaters fill in when there is a vacancy, until the position is filled.

Working as a floater secretary can be extremely challenging, since you never know what you may be doing or whom you may be working for. Usually, floaters have excellent secretarial skills and some previous law firm experience. Working as a floater is an excellent way to gain experience in many different areas of a law firm. Some people choose to work as a floater until they decide which area in a firm they want to work in.

Entry-Level Secretaries

Working as an entry-level secretary is a great way to gain experience and work your way into an experienced legal secretarial position. I'm talking about an entry-level secretarial position that doesn't require previous legal or even secretarial experience. You may find these positions in smaller firms where they can't afford to pay for someone with many years of legal experience. Finding someone who is willing to give you an initial opportunity is your biggest obstacle. If you can't find someone who is willing to give you a chance, you might have to work as a temporary first, demonstrating your ability and positive attitude firsthand. I know I sound like a broken record, but use your networking skills to find someone who's willing to give you a chance as an entry-level secretary.

I encountered one secretary during my law firm years who found an attorney who was willing to give her a chance. She had no previous experience and recently graduated from a two-year post–high school program. All she really had going for her was her great attitude. She came across a partner who didn't want to pay high legal secretarial rates, so he hired her.

She wasn't the best secretary I ever came across, but what she lacked in technical skills, she made up for everywhere else. She ultimately developed a strong bond with her partner boss, and when she decided to relocate to the West Coast, the partner helped her find a new position. A good attitude and the willingness to succeed can go a very long way.

Receptionists

Receptionist positions in law firms are another job that many people tend to overlook. Most firms have at least one receptionist position, and others may employ numerous people in this position if they occupy many floors or have different shifts. If a receptionist position suits your fancy, a law firm is an excellent place to be one. Law firm receptionists, however, are usually very professional, and some have multiple language capabilities.

This job, in a law firm, differs little from receptionist positions in other industries. However, you may find that firms are combining this position with other jobs. For example, the receptionist may have a computer terminal on his or her desk and may have the additional responsibility of data entry, accounts receivable, or composing an internal newsletter. The combinations of responsibilities are numerous.

General Clerks

Last, but certainly not least, are general clerks. I am referring to the gofers, grunts, couriers, or whatever a firm chooses to call them. These are the people who do all the other tasks in law firms. These are the tasks that usually fall to the bottom of the barrel, the ones that no one likes to do—making deliveries, cleaning up after conferences, moving furniture, sorting mail, delivering mail and faxes, sending faxes, and so on. Someone has to fill in the holes.

Clerk positions aren't glamorous by any means, but they are good jobs for someone between jobs or for someone who is still trying to figure out where to go next.

23

THE FUTURE OF LAW FIRM RECRUITING

The past keeps getting bigger and bigger at the future's expense.
—TENNESSEE WILLIAMS

What does the future look like for law firm recruiting? What will the job picture look like for recent law school graduates, experienced attorneys, legal administrators, and support personnel in the coming years? No one knows for sure, but I'll make a few predictions of my own, based on my years of experience in law firm recruiting.

1. *Recruiting will continue to stabilize, and small firms will continue to hire more students than the large ones.* I think that law firm recruiting will continue to stay on its current path for at the least the immediate future. During the last few years, there have been few significant changes in the number of students getting into firms. As in the rest of the economy, the smaller firms will continue to hire more people than the large ones. While the glory days of the 1980s are gone for good, I think we'll have a steady employment picture for the immediate future.

2. *Big firms will continue to hire only from the best schools.* It would surprise me if the big firms altered their paths and started going to lesser-known schools or started to dip down lower into classes by lowering their academic standards. Law firms are just too ingrained in their thinking. The Ivy Leaguers want more Ivy Leaguers.

3. *It's going to get tougher for the bottom of the class.* We're beginning to see a polarization in the employment world—there's a gap between those who have fabulous credentials and are willing to make huge sacrifices for work and those who have average or below-average credentials and want to work nine to five. I think you're going to see this polarization in the legal world, too.

4. *More law graduates will work outside of law firms in nonlegal positions.* This trend has already begun. More lawyers will work in more nontradi-

tional jobs, or they'll leave law firms eventually. Many people are becoming disenchanted with the legal profession, and others are in it who should have never entered it in the first place. I think that as more generation Xers start graduating from law school, their choices will be different from those of the baby boomers.

5. *Law firms will ultimately have to face diversity issues.* As the Hudson Institute's report *Workforce 2000* reminds us, our workforce is going to be more diverse with time. Law firms, which tend to lag behind the times on these kinds of issues, will eventually have to make changes in the way they recruit in order to hire a more diverse group of attorneys. At present, they're light-years away from grappling with this issue. Those firms that face the music sooner will have much better success in recruiting our diverse attorney population. Student members of this diverse population will also have to wrestle with an industry that hasn't gone through puberty on this issue.

6. *Support personnel will continue to face a rosy employment picture.* Those in legal support positions, especially paralegal, marketing, and computer professionals, will have an ample supply of jobs available to them in the future. I think you'll also see more J.D.s joining the ranks of the administrators once they figure out that these aren't terrible positions after all. And as the Hudson Institute's study indicates, it is anticipated that service positions will far outstrip opportunities in other fields into the next decade.

7. *Technology will change legal recruiting.* We're starting to see how the Internet and World Wide Web can be used in recruiting. Having access and being able to "surf the Net and the Web" will become crucial to any job search in the near future, in any field. Technology will make the recruiting process much faster, and your ability to present yourself on paper or on screen will become even more important than it is today. On-campus recruiting, as we know it today, may cease to exist.

8. *The jobs will be in the smaller firms.* Again, as we are starting to see today, the real growth will be in the small firms. More and more jobs, for all types of personnel, will be in these firms. Finding these positions will continue to be difficult, and networking will be even more important than it is today.

Making predictions about the future of anything is a tricky business, and we're often wrong in our prophesies. To prove my point, I recently came across an article I had cut from a magazine in 1980 that declared that after the decadence of the 1970s, the 1980s would be a time for abstinence. In fact, the article was entitled, "The Joy of Abstinence." To keep from embarrassing the author, I won't reveal her name. But my point is that no one really knows for sure what the future holds for any industry, especially one that has been on a roller-coaster ride in recent times like the legal profession. The primary purpose is not to make predictions, but to help you to understand how the legal recruiting process works so that perhaps you, too, can anticipate what to do next. Think about what you want out of life, plan for it, set goals for yourself, and then go out and achieve them. The legal profession has much to offer those who are suited for it and those who go about getting into it through a well-planned effort.

APPENDIX

NALP "PRINCIPLES AND STANDARDS FOR LAW PLACEMENT AND RECRUITMENT ACTIVITIES"

Introduction

The National Association for Law Placement (NALP) was organized in 1971 to promote the exchange of information and cooperation between law schools and employers. In order to advance those interests, the Association has developed these "Principles and Standards for Law Placement and Recruitment Activities."

The NALP "Principles and Standards for Law Placement and Recruitment Activities" were first adopted in 1978. Part V, "General Standards for the Timing of Offers and Decisions," was derived from "Interviewing Procedures for Law Students and Prospective Employers," a set of guidelines originally adopted in the early 1960s by a group of law schools meeting under the auspices of the Association of the Bar of the City of New York. Subsequent modifications were adopted in 1985, 1988, 1992, and 1994.

The "Principles and Standards for Law Placement and Recruitment Activities" are organized as follows:

I. General Principles
II. Principles for Law Schools
III. Principles for Candidates
IV. Principles for Employers
V. General Standards for the Timing of Offers and Decisions

NALP encourages law schools and legal employers to educate all participants in the law placement and recruitment process about the spirit and the letter of these "Principles and Standards." NALP urges all participants in the law student recruitment process, including members and non-members of NALP, to abide by these "Principles and Standards."

Part I. General Principles

Successful recruitment and placement of law students requires cooperation and good judgment from three groups—law schools, candidates, and employers. These "Principles and Standards" provide concrete guidelines for each group. Nothing in the "Principles and Standards" is intended to alter any legal relationships among the participants, but participants are urged to carry out all obligations in good faith.

Activities related to the placement and hiring of law students should be conducted on the highest ethical and professional level. Timely exchange of accurate information is essential.

Recruitment activities should be scheduled so as to minimize interference with students' academic work.

Underlying these guidelines for ethical behavior is NALP's fundamental commit-

Reprinted with permission of National Association for Law Placement, Suite 325, 1666 Connecticut Avenue, NW, Washington, DC 20009-1039.

ment to the accessibility of the legal profession to all individuals of competence and requisite moral character. NALP is strongly opposed to discrimination which is based upon gender, age, race, color, religious creed, national origin, physical disability, marital, parental or veteran status, sexual orientation, or the prejudice of clients related to such matters.

In addition to abiding by these guidelines, all parties concerned with placement and hiring should observe strictly all relevant laws, accreditation standards and institutional policies. A law school may deny use of its placement facilities to students and employers who fail to adhere to these "Principles and Standards." If unusual circumstances or particular organizational constraints require a law school, a candidate, or an employer to modify any provision herein, every effort should be made to find an alternative acceptable to all parties concerned.

Part II. Principles for Law Schools

A. *Law schools should make career planning and placement services available to all students.*

1. Career planning and placement are integral parts of legal education. Law schools should dedicate to them adequate physical space, equipment, financial support, and staff.
2. The professional services of a career planning and placement office should be available to students without charge.
3. Law schools should strive to meet the placement needs and interests of all students. Preferential treatment should not be extended to any student or employer.

B. *Law schools should subscribe to and promote practices that protect their students' legal rights.*

1. Law schools should articulate and publish meaningful policies prohibiting discriminatory hiring practices. Procedures should be developed and published whereby claims of violations can be investigated and resolved promptly and fairly.
2. Students' privacy should be protected against illegal or inappropriate dissemination of personal information. Information protected by federal, state, or municipal law must not be disclosed without proper consent. Institutional policies conforming to prevailing laws should be formulated and published to the attention of both students and employers.

C. *Law schools should educate students as to proper career investigation techniques and protocol.*

1. Publications and counseling provided by law schools should be designed to afford students adequate information about the variety of opportunities available to persons with legal training and proper methods for exploring such opportunities.
2. Students should be counseled to focus their career choices based on their aptitudes and career goals.

D. *Students' freedom of choice in career decisions should be protected from undue influences.*

1. In counseling students, placement officers and others within the law school community should avoid interposing either their own values or institutional interests.

2. Law schools should disseminate "Part V: General Standards for the Timing of Offers and Decisions" to students and employers and urge all participants in the law student recruitment process, including members and nonmembers of NALP, to adhere to them so that students can make informed decisions.

E. *Law schools should develop and maintain productive working relationships with a broad range of employers.*

1. Law schools should work actively to develop and maintain employment opportunities for students and graduates. All employment opportunity notices should be publicized to all students.

2. To enhance student learning and increase career development opportunities, the office of career services should maintain good working relationships with students, faculty, alumnae/i, and other elements of the legal community.

3. In order to ensure maximum information-sharing and efficiency in the placement process, law schools should cooperate with one another to the fullest extent possible in gathering employer information and providing interview services.

4. Law schools should not disseminate information learned in confidence from employers.

F. *Law schools should establish adequate procedures to facilitate recruitment by employers.*

1. Procedures to enable employers to conduct on-campus interviews, solicit direct applications or collect student resumes should be designed for maximum efficiency and fairness. Those procedures should be clearly articulated and available in writing to students and employers.

2. In dealing with employers, law schools should make maximum use of standardized forms and procedures.

G. *Law schools should establish and implement practices to ensure the fair and accurate representation of students and the institution in the placement process.*

1. Law schools should adopt and enforce policies that prohibit misrepresentation and other student abuses of the employment search process, such as engaging in interviews for practice, holding more than four offers, failing to decline offers in which there is no longer interest, or continuing to interview after acceptance of employment.

2. Law schools should provide to employers and other interested parties comprehensive information on grade standards and distribution, curriculum, degree requirements, admissions and enrollment profiles, academic awards criteria, and office of career services policies and procedures.

3. NALP *Employment and Salary Survey* information should be collected by law schools and the survey results made available to employers, prospective students, and all other interested parties.

Part III. Principles for Candidates

A. *Candidates should prepare thoroughly for the employment search process.*

1. Before beginning an employment search, candidates should engage in

thorough self-examination. Work skills, vocational aptitudes and interests, lifestyle and geographic preferences, academic performance, career expectations and life experiences should be carefully evaluated so that informed choices can be made. General instruction should be obtained on employment search skills, particularly those relating to the interview process.

2. Prior to making employment inquiries, candidates should learn as much as possible about target employers and the nature of their positions. Candidates should interview only with employers in whom they have a genuine interest.

3. Candidates should comply with the placement policies and procedures of law schools whose services they use.

B. **Throughout the employment search process candidates should represent their qualifications and interests fully and accurately.**

1. Candidates should be prepared to provide, at employers' request, copies of all academic transcripts. Under no circumstances should academic biographical data be falsified, misrepresented, or distorted either in writing or orally. Candidates who engage in such conduct may be subject to elimination from consideration for employment by the employer, suspension or other academic discipline by the law school, and disqualification from admission to practice by bar admission authorities.

2. Candidates should be prepared to advise prospective employers of the nature and extent of their training in legal writing. Writing samples submitted as evidence of a candidate's legal skills should be wholly original work. Where the writing was done with others, the candidate's contribution should be

clearly identified. Writing samples from law-related employment must be masked adequately to preserve client confidentiality and used only with the permission of the supervising attorney.

C. **Throughout the employment search process students should conduct themselves in a professional manner.**

1. Candidates who participate in the on-campus interview process should adhere to all scheduling commitments. Cancellations should occur only for good cause and should be promptly communicated to the office of career services or the employer.

2. Invitations for in-office interviews should be acknowledged promptly and accepted only if the candidate has a genuine interest in the employer.

3. Candidates should reach an understanding with the employer regarding its reimbursement policies prior to the trip. Expenses for trips during which interviews with more than one employer occur should be prorated in accordance with those employers' reimbursement policies.

4. Candidates invited to interview at employer offices should request reimbursement for reasonable expenses that are directly related to the interview and incurred in good faith. Failure to observe this policy, or faisification or misrepresentation of travel expenses, may result in non-reimbursement and elimination from consideration for employment or the revocation of offers by an employer.

D. **Candidates should notify employers and their office of career services of their acceptance or rejection of employment offers by the earliest possible time, and no later than the time** *established by rule, custom, or agreement.*

1. Candidates should expect offers to be confirmed in writing. Candidates should abide by the standards for student responses set out in Part V and should in any event notify the employers as soon as their decision is made, even if that decision is made in advance of the prevailing deadline date.

2. In fairness to both employers and peers, students should act in good faith to decline promptly offers for interviews and employment which are no longer being seriously considered. In order for law schools to comply with federal and institutional reporting requirements, students should notify the office of career services upon acceptance of an employment offer, whether or not the employment was obtained through the office.

3. Candidates seeking or preparing to accept fellowships, judicial clerkships, or other limited term professional employment should apprise prospective employers of their intentions and obtain a clear understanding of their offer deferral policies.

E. *Candidates should honor their employment commitments.*

1. Candidates should, upon acceptance of an offer of employment, notify their office of career services and notify all employers who consider them to be active candidates that they have accepted a position.

2. If, because of extraordinary and unforeseen circumstances, it becomes necessary for a candidate to modify or be released from his or her acceptance, both the employer and the office of career services should be notified promptly.

F. *Candidates should promptly report to the office of career services any misrepresentation, discrimination or other abuse by employers in the employment process.*

G. *Students who engage in law-related employment should adhere to the same standards of conduct as lawyers.*

1. In matters arising out of law-related employment, students should be guided by the standards for professional conduct which are applicable in the employer's state. When acting on behalf of employers in a recruitment capacity, students should be guided by the employer principles in Part IV.

2. Students should exercise care to provide full and fair information when advising peers about former employers.

Part IV. Principles for Employers

A. *Employers should maintain productive working relationships with law schools.*

1. Employers should inform the law school office of career services in advance of any recruiting activities involving their students, whether conducted on- or off-campus, and should, at the conclusion of those activities, inform the office of career services of the results obtained.

2. Employers without formal recruiting programs or whose hiring activities are sporadic in nature should notify the law school office of career services as far in advance as possible of planned recruiting activities in order that appropriate assistance might be arranged.

3. Employers who conduct on-campus interviews should refrain from making

unnecessary schedule change requests.

B. Employers should respect the policies, procedures and legal obligations of individual law schools and should request only services or information that are consistent therewith.

1. Employers should not expect or request preferential services from law schools.
2. Employers should not solicit information received by law schools in confidence from candidates or other employers.
3. Appointments with candidates for in-house interviews should be established for a mutually convenient time so as not to unduly disrupt students' studies.
4. Employers should promptly report to the office of career services any misrepresentation or other abuse by students of the employment search process.

C. Employers should provide full and accurate information about the organization and the positions for which recruitment is being conducted.

1. Employers should provide to law schools complete organizational information as contained in the NALP Employer Questionnaire, well in advance of any recruitment activities. Position descriptions should include information about the qualifications sought in candidates, the hiring timetable, nature of the work, the number of available positions, and, if known at the time, the starting salary to be offered.
2. Invitations for in-office interviews should include a clear explanation of all expense reimbursement policies and procedures.

D. Employer organizations are responsible for the conduct of their recruiters

and for any representation made by them.

1. Employers should designate recruiters who are both skilled and knowledgeable about the employing organization.
2. Employers should instruct interviewers not to make any unauthorized commitments.
3. Candidates personal privacy should be safeguarded. Information about candidates that is protected by law should not be disclosed by an employer to any third party without specific permission.

E. Employers should use valid, job related criteria when evaluating candidates.

1. Hiring decisions must be based solely on bona fide occupational qualifications. Employers should carefully avoid conduct of any kind during the interview and selection process that acts or appears to act to discriminate unlawfully or in a way contrary to the policies of a particular institution.
2. Factors in candidates' backgrounds that have no predictive value with respect to employment performance, such as scores on examinations required for admission to academic institutions, should not be relied upon by employers in the hiring process.
3. When evaluating second and third year applicants, employers should not place undue emphasis on the nature of a first year summer job experience or on a student's decision not to work after the first year.
4. There has been a long-standing tradition that the first year summer be used to engage in public service work or to take time away from the law altogether, and, while the practice of having first year students work in private law firms provides additional employ-

ment opportunities to some students, such experiences should not be valued or emphasized inordinately.

F. *Employers should refrain from any activity that may adversely affect the ability of candidates to make an independent and considered decision.*

1. Employers should give candidates a reasonable period of time to consider offers of employment and should avoid conduct that subjects candidates to undue pressure to accept.
2. Response deadlines should be established when the offer of employment is made. Employers who extend offers in the fall should abide by the timetable for student response set out in Part V and must abide by it with respect to students enrolled in law schools that have adopted it as an employer requirement.
3. Employers should not offer special inducements to persuade candidates to accept offers of employment earlier than is customary or prescribed under the circumstances.

G. *An employer should honor all commitments made on its behalf.*

1. Offers of employment should be made in writing, with all terms clearly expressed.
2. If, because of extraordinary and unforeseen circumstances, it becomes necessary for an employer to rescind or modify an offer of employment, both the student and the office of career services should be notified promptly.

Part V: General Standards for the Timing of Offers and Decisions

To promote fair and ethical practices for the interviewing and decision-making process, NALP offers the following standards for the timing of offers and decisions:

A. *General Provisions*

1. All offers to law students should remain open for at least two weeks after the date made unless the offers are made pursuant to Paragraphs B and C below, in which case the later response date should apply.
2. Law students should reaffirm offers governed by Paragraphs B and C below within thirty days from the date of the offer letter. Employers may retract any offer that is not reaffirmed by the student.
3. Students are expected to accept or release offers or negotiate an extension of the response date by the applicable deadline.
4. After October 15, a student should not hold open more than four offers of employment simultaneously, and after November 1, a student should not hold open more than three offers simultaneously, including offers received as a result of previous summer employment. For each offer received that places a student over the offer limit, the student should, within one week of receipt of the excess offer, release an offer.
5. Second and third year students may, with the consent of the employer, extend one offer beyond December 1.
6. Employers should promptly report offers and decisions through NALPOfrs.
7. Employers having a total of 25 attorneys or fewer in all offices may be exempted from Paragraphs B and C below but should leave offers open for a minimum of two weeks.
8. Employers offering part-time or temporary positions for the school term may be exempted from the requirements of Paragraphs B and C below.

9. Violations of these guidelines should be reported to the student's career services office.

B. Full-Time Employment Provisions

1. Employers offering full-time positions following graduation to law students not previously employed by them should leave those offers open at least until December 1.

2. Employers making offers **before** September 15 of the student's third year for full-time positions following graduation to law students previously employed by them during any preceding summer should leave those offers open at least until November 1. Upon request by the student, an employer should extend this date until December 1 upon receipt of assurances from the student that he or she is holding and will hold no more than one other offer during the extension period.

3. Employers making offers **on or after** September 15 of the student's third year for full-time employment following graduation to law students previously employed by them during any preceding summer should leave those offers open at least until December 1.

C. Summer Employment Provisions for Second and Third Year Students

1. Employers offering summer positions in the fall to law students not previously employed by them should leave those offers open at least until December 1.

2. Employers making offers **before** September 15 for a second summer clerkship to law students previously employed by them during any preceding summer should leave those offers open at least until November 1. Upon request by the student, an employer should extend this date until December 1 upon receipt of assurances from the student that he or she is holding and will hold no more than one other offer during the extension period.

3. Employers making offers **on or after** September 15 for a second summer clerkship to law students previously employed by them during any preceding summer should leave those offers open at least until December 1.

D. Summer Employment Provisions for First Year Students

1. Law schools should not offer placement services to first semester first year law students prior to November 1 except in the case of part-time students who may be given assistance in seeking positions during the school term.

2. Prospective employers and first year law students should not initiate contact with one another and employers should not interview or make offers to first year students before December 1.

3. All offers to first year students for summer employment should remain open for at least two weeks after the date made.

INDEX

ABOUT THE AUTHOR

Ann Turnicky was born in Raleigh, North Carolina, and grew up in nearby Winston-Salem, North Carolina. She received her bachelor of arts degree from Salem College and her master's degree in business administration from Johns Hopkins University in Baltimore, Maryland. She lives in Brookeville, Maryland, just outside Washington, D.C., with her husband, Ron.

She was the recruiting director for Petree Stockton & Robinson (now Kilpatrick Stockton), a large regional law firm with offices throughout the Southeast for four years. At Petree Stockton & Robinson, she established the firm's first professional recruiting program. After departing North Carolina, she became the director of recruiting and professional development for the Washington, D.C., office of Baker & McKenzie, a position she held for more than five years. While at Baker & McKenzie, she established the office's first formal professional recruiting program and worked with numerous offices of the firm, both domestically and internationally.

Ms. Turnicky has been a regular contributor to legal recruiting and marketing journals and has lectured at local, regional, and national meetings and to student groups on legal recruiting related topics. She currently is establishing a recruiting program for an engineering, training, and technical services company with offices throughout the United States and abroad. Ms. Turnicky continues to write on legal, business, and marketing related topics for companies and law firms throughout the United States.